great little gifts
to
knit

great little gifts to knit

30 QUICK AND COLORFUL PATTERNS

Jean Moss

The Taunton Press

T The Taunton Press

The Taunton Press, Inc., 63 South Main Street,
PO Box 5506, Newtown, CT 06470-5506
e-mail: tp@taunton.com

Editor: RENEE IWASZKIEWICZ NEIGER
Technical editor: ASHLEY LITTLE
Copy editor: BETTY CHRISTIANSEN
Indexer: JAY KREIDER
Cover design: MICHELLE THOMPSON |
FOLD & GATHER DESIGN
Interior design: ALISON WILKES
Layout: CATHY CASSIDY
Illustrators: JEAN MOSS
and CHRISTINE ERIKSON
Photographer: BURCU AVSAR
Photo editor: ERIN GIUNTA
Location: ALMS & TERRA, BEACON, NY
Prop Stylist: ELIZABETH MACLENNAN
Baby model: OLIVER KICKEL
Toddler model: EDIE GIUNTA

The following names/manufacturers
appearing in *Great Little Gifts to Knit*
are trademarks: Rowan®, Velcro®.
Standard Yarn Weight System (p. 126)
and Needle and Hook Sizing
information (p. 129) courtesy of the
Craft Yarn Council,
www.yarnstandards.com

Library of Congress
Cataloging-in-Publication Data in progress

ISBN 978-1-60085-847-5

Printed in the United States of America
10 9 8 7 6 5 4 3 2 1

Dedication

For givers of gifts everywhere,
for you make the world a better place.

Also for the men in my life, for you have given me
the gift of seeing the other side of things.

Acknowledgments

My love and thanks go to one and all who have worked on this book.

I've often heard it said that something is greater than the sum of its parts, and if that should be the case with this book, it'll be a cracker for sure. I'm so lucky to find myself working with a whole galaxy of talented people.

There are four who have been especially important: Ann Banks, Jenny Metcalfe, Rita Taylor, and Margaret Race. They are my sample knitters, who have tried and tested every stitch.

Ann and Ruth at Wensleydale Longwool Sheepshop sent me colorful samples of their hand-dyed fleece, and over the years they have plied me with many cups of tea in Ann's kitchen on visits to the farm with our knitters' tours.

Rowan Yarns' gorgeous fibers shine through in every project: Vicky Sedgwick has been a rock in sending out the sample yarns so efficiently.

Debbie Abrahams and her husband, Steve, went the extra mile, sending my beads promptly, one time even whilst on holiday.

Shawna Mullen originally suggested the idea of *Great Little Gifts to Knit*. She is an inspiring editor who knows how to bring out the best in people.

Renee Neiger has supervised this project throughout, skillfully assisted by technical editor Ashley Little. Both did a great job with their thorough and thoughtful edits.

Burcu Avsar's cool and sophisticated images leap out from the pages, expressing perfectly the spirit of the gift.

Philip Mercer leaves no stone unturned, making sure nothing is forgotten.

Finally, I must thank my family and friends, who do an excellent job of keeping my feet firmly on the ground, reminding me *it's only knitting!*

Contents

Introduction

THIS BOOK IS TOTALLY NEW GROUND FOR ME. NEVER BEFORE HAVE I done a book of small projects. My previous book, *Sweet Shawlettes*, is a book of accessories and was not that much of a departure from my usual collections of sweaters.

However, with *Great Little Gifts to Knit*, every project is totally different, making the book from the outset an unknown voyage of discovery for me—in fact, a teeny bit scary. If I'd known then what a delight it was to become, I wouldn't have been worried at all. My only regret is that time constraints prevented me from exploring each path to its natural creative end. However, whenever possible, I've included extra colorways and different yarn options to further illustrate the potential of each project.

The idea of creating a book of gifts is something that appeals to my overactive sense of celebration. Births, engagements, weddings, namings, housewarmings, anniversaries—even funerals—can celebrate a life and help us remember all the things we loved about a person. Gatherings and parties remind us of the good things in life and give a sense of perspective to the difficult times. Giving makes you feel good, and this feeling of well-being allows you to relax and regenerate, opening up new possibilities for the future.

The book is arranged into four chapters, each relating to the recipients of the gifts. Some are personal favorites I've previously

knitted for family and friends, but the majority are brand-new designs, chosen because they're ones I would love to give or receive. In **Baby**, you'll find booties, hats, mittens, cocoons, a blanket, and a toddler jacket. I've gone to town in **Hers**, with amulet purses, fingerless gloves, a shrug, leg warmers, a turban, a hat, a beret, zebra mittens, a stole, a shawlette, and a backpack. **His** offers socks, a hat, a head wrap, a guitar strap, a belt, a scarf, and a smartphone cover. The collection's rounded off with **Home**, comprising cushion covers, seat covers, place mats, napkin rings, a doggie jacket, tea cozies, and a celebratory toran or door hanging.

No matter how long you've been knitting—whether a month or a lifetime—there are projects for all skill levels. Many projects are mini workshops in certain knit techniques—great for expanding your portfolio while working on something useful.

And never underestimate the value of good yarn so buy the best you can afford. I've used Rowan because I love it and I know it so well, which helps me along in the design process. That said, don't worry if you can't source the exact yarn. If you can roughly match the yardage and have checked that gauge and hand are compatible by swatching, there's no reason why you shouldn't use an alternative.

And please don't forget to ask for help at your local yarn store. They provide a unique opportunity to discuss projects, help you make the right yarn choices, and guide you through the sometimes choppy sea of yarn substitution.

I hope *Great Little Gifts to Knit* will bring you many hours of enjoyable knitting and that your gifts will be loved by all who receive them. My wish is that your creativity and generosity will be rewarded, not in the financial sense, but by the warm glow of satisfaction that comes from making beautiful handmade gifts, heirloom pieces for friends and family to enjoy and cherish.

—Jean Moss

CHAPTER 1

Baby

OUR FAMILY TREE HAS ACQUIRED A NEW SET OF BRANCHES over the past five years. To much excitement, the grandbabies started to arrive, bringing into focus a whole new set of possibilities for gifts.

Tiny knits have been flowing from my needles—for birthdays and holidays, but mainly because I love making them. I've knit every pattern in this chapter, with multiples of some, enjoying every minute. A tiny hat can be finished in an evening. Knit with ultrasoft yarn and lovingly wrapped, what better gift could a new parent receive?

The projects cover a wide range of skills, from easy to advanced. For the beginner, there's the hat, mitts, and booties combo of **Shower Set**, and I've also included a simple version of the snuggly, ribbed **Cuddle Cocoon**. The intermediate knitter will have no problems tackling the **Baby Love Blanket** and the colorful intarsia of the **Whoopla Beanbags**. And the **Jubilee Jacket and Hat** is the perfect project to keep the more experienced knitter happy.

Showcased techniques include shadow knitting, intarsia, Fair Isle, chart reading, circular knitting, and twisted stitches. Finishing includes mitered corners, knots, tassels, knit flowers, and single crochet.

Cuddle Cocoon

This is the perfect gift for welcoming a new baby into the world. There are two alternatives here, a straight ribbed version for the beginner and a swirl rib for the more experienced knitter. Worked in the round for seamless comfort, it's guaranteed to ensure little ones are kept snug and warm during those first few months. And there's a bonus: the medium size makes a fabulous gift for mom. Just work 6 in. (15 cm) straight, then work the decreases—*et voilà*, a matching hat!

SKILL LEVEL
Beginner/Intermediate

TIME TO KNIT
Weekend

FINISHED MEASUREMENTS
Extra-Extra-Small: 19 in. (48.25 cm) long, 12 in. (30.5 cm) in diameter
Extra-Small: 21 in. (53.5 cm) long, 15 in. (38 cm) in diameter
Small: 23 in. (58.5 cm) long, 17 in. (43 cm) in diameter
Medium: 25 in. (63.5 cm) long, 19 in. (49 cm) in diameter
Large: 28 in. (71 cm) long, 22 in. (56 cm) in diameter
Extra-Large: 30 in. (76.25 cm) long, 24 in. (61 cm) in diameter

Note
Pattern is written for size Extra-Extra-Small, with Extra-Small, Small, Medium, Large, and Extra-Large instructions in parentheses where necessary.

YARN
Rowan® Big Wool
87 yd. (80 m) per 100 g ball:
2 balls Glamour 036 or Vert 054

NOTIONS
Set of 4 size 13 U.S. (9 mm) double-pointed needles
Size 13 U.S. (9 mm) 24-in. circular needle *or size to obtain gauge*
Size K-10 U.S. (6.5 mm) crochet hook
Stitch markers
Tapestry needle

GAUGE
13 sts and 14 rows = 4 in. (10 cm) in K2, P2 Rib

SPECIAL ABBREVIATION
RT
K2tog but do not slip from needle. Insert RH needle between the sts just knitted tog and knit the first stitch again, then slip both sts together.

TO MAKE COCOON
Advanced Version (shown on the facing page)
Using circular needle, cast on 40 (48, 56, 64, 72, 80) sts. Do not join in the round.
Row 1 (WS) Sl 1, k1, *p2, k2; rep from * to last 2 sts, p1, k1tbl.
Row 2 Sl 1, k1, *p2, RT; rep from * to last 2 sts, p1, k1tbl.
Row 3 Sl 1, k1, *k1, p2, k1; rep from * to last 2 sts, k1, k1tbl.
Row 4 Sl 1, *p2, RT; rep from * to last 3 sts, p2, k1tbl.
Row 5 Sl 1, p1, *k2, p2; rep from * to last 2 sts, k1, k1tbl.
Row 6 Sl 1, p1, *RT, p2; rep from * to last 2 sts, k1, k1tbl.
Row 7 Sl 1, p2, *k2, p2; rep from * to last st, k1tbl.
Row 8 Sl 1, *RT, p2; rep from * to last 3 sts, RT, k1tbl.

continued on page 10

The Beginner Version in Vert.

Work these 8 rows twice, then work the first 3 rows—19 rows. Work should measure 5 in. (12.75 cm) from cast-on edge.
Cut yarn and turn work so that RS is facing.
Begin working in the round:
Round 1 Sl 2 sts to RH needle, reattach yarn, and pm. *P1, RT, p1; rep from * around, finishing with the 2 slipped sts.
Round 2 *P1, k2, p1; rep from * to last 4 sts, k1, p2.

Note
The last st becomes the first st of the next round. The beginning of the round moves backward by 1 st every other round. Adjust marker accordingly.

Rep round 1 (from *) and round 2 until work measures 16½ (18½, 20½, 22½, 25½, 27½) in. [42 (47, 52, 57, 64.75, 70) cm] from cast-on edge, ending on round 2.

Base of cocoon
Round 1 *P1, RT, p2tog, RT, p1, pm; rep from * 4 (5, 6, 7, 8, 9) more times.
Round 2 *P1, k2, p1, k2, p1, sm; rep from * to last 7 sts, p1, k2, p1, k2 (the last st will be worked with the first st of next round).

Round 3 *P1, RT, p2tog, k1, p1; rep from * 4 (5, 6, 7, 8, 9) more times.
Round 4 *P1, k1, p2, k1, p1, sm; rep from * to last 6 sts, p1, k1, p2, k1 (the last st will be worked with the first st of next round).
Round 5 *P1, RT, p2tog, k1, sm; rep from * 4 (5, 6, 7, 8, 9) more times.
Round 6 *P1, k1, p2tog, k1, sm; rep from * 4 (5, 6, 7, 8, 9) more times.
Round 7 *P1, k1, k2tog, sm; rep from * 4 (5, 6, 7, 8, 9) more times.
Round 8 *K2tog, k1, sm; rep from * 4 (5, 6, 7, 8, 9) more times.
Round 9 *K2tog, sm; rep from * around— 5 (6, 7, 8, 9, 10) sts.
Thread tapestry needle through rem 5 (6, 7, 8, 9, 10) sts, pull tightly, and secure.

Beginner Version (photo at left)
Using circular needle, cast on 40 (48, 56, 64, 72, 80) sts. Do not join in the round.
Row 1 (RS) Sl 1, k1, *p2, k2; rep from * to last 2 sts, p1, k1tbl.
Row 2 Sl 1, k1, *p2, k2; rep from * to last 2 sts, p1, k1tbl.
Rep rows 1 and 2 until 18 rows have been worked. Work should measure 5 in. (12.75 cm) from cast-on edge.
Begin working in the round:
Round 1 Place first 2 sts on LH needle, pm, *p2, k2; rep from * to end, including the 2 sts from beg of row.
Round 2 *P2, k2; rep from * around.
Rep round 2 until work measures 16½ (18½, 20½, 22½, 25½, 27½) in. [42 (47, 52, 57, 64.75, 70) cm] from cast-on edge.

Base of cocoon
Round 1 *P2, k2, p2tog, k2, pm; rep from * 4 (5, 6, 7, 8, 9) more times.
Round 2 *P2, k2, p1, k2, sm; rep from * 4 (5, 6, 7, 8, 9) more times.
Round 3 *P2, k2, k2tog, k1, sm; rep from * 4 (5, 6, 7, 8, 9) more times.
Round 4 *P2, k4, sm; rep from * 4 (5, 6, 7, 8, 9) more times.

Cuddle Schematic

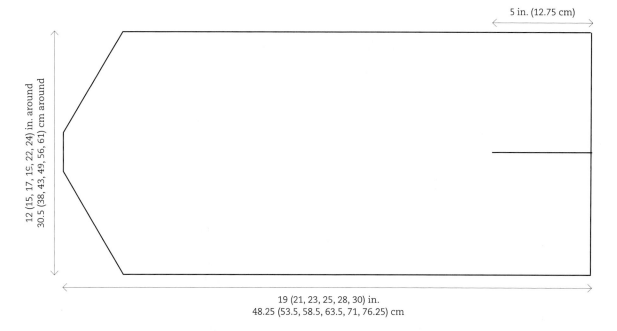

5 in. (12.75 cm)

12 (15, 17, 19, 22, 24) in. around
30.5 (38, 43, 49, 56, 61) cm around

19 (21, 23, 25, 28, 30) in.
48.25 (53.5, 58.5, 63.5, 71, 76.25) cm

Round 5 *P2, k2, k2tog, sm; rep from *
4 (5, 6, 7, 8, 9) more times.
Round 6 *P2, k1, k2tog, sm; rep from *
4 (5, 6, 7, 8, 9) more times.
Round 7 *P2, k2tog, sm; rep from *
4 (5, 6, 7, 8, 9) more times.
Round 8 *P2tog, k1, sm; rep from *
4 (5, 6, 7, 8, 9) more times.
Round 9 *K2tog, sm; rep from *
around—5 (6, 7, 8, 9, 10) sts.
Thread tapestry needle through the rem 5
(6, 7, 8, 9, 10) sts on needle, pull tightly, and secure.

FINISHING (BOTH VERSIONS)
Block lightly on WS.
Starting at center front, work 1 round
sc (p. 122) around neck edge.

TO MAKE HAT
Advanced Version (p. 8)
Using dpns, cast on 40 sts. Distribute sts evenly
on 3 needles. Join in the round, taking care not to
twist sts.
Round 1 *P1, RT, p1; rep from * around.
Round 2 *P1, k2, p1; rep from * to last 4 sts, k1, p2—
the last st becomes the first st of the next round.

Note
*The beginning of the round moves backward by 1 st
every other round. Adjust marker accordingly.*

Rep rounds 1 and 2 until work measures 2 in.
(5 cm) from cast-on edge, ending on round 2.
Work 9 rows for base of hat the same as for base
of cocoon, with 4 reps of the pattern on each row.
Thread tapestry needle through rem sts and
gather tightly. Secure the yarn on the inside.

Beginner Version (p. 10)
Using dpns, cast on 40 sts. Distribute sts evenly
on 3 needles. Join in the round, taking care not
to twist sts.
Round 1 *P2, k2; rep from * around.
Rep round 1 until work measures 1½ in. (4 cm)
from cast-on edge. If necessary, adjust length
to fit baby's head.
For base of hat, work 9 rounds the same as for base
of cocoon, with 4 reps of the pattern on each row.
Thread tapestry needle through rem sts and gather
tightly. Secure the yarn on the inside.

Shower Set

As a proud grandmother of four, I've had plenty of practice knitting for newborns and know that the extremities are important to keep out of the cold. So projects that cover head, hands, and feet are the ones that make excellent gifts. Until very recently, I've been knitting for granddaughters, so this set has a definite gender bias. To make the set for a boy, trim each piece with turquoise or navy and omit the flower on the hat and slippers.

SKILL LEVEL
Beginner

TIME TO KNIT
Weekend

FINISHED MEASUREMENTS
(To fit newborn to 3 months)
Hat: 10-in. (25.5 cm) circumference
Slippers: 3 in. (9.5 cm) long
Mittens: 4 in. (11.5 cm) long

YARN
Rowan Cashsoft DK
126 yd. (115 m) per 50 g ball:
2 balls Lime 509 (A)
1 ball Sky Pink 540 (B)

NOTIONS
Set of 4 size 3 U.S. (3.25 mm)
double-pointed needles
Set of 4 size 6 U.S. (4 mm)
double-pointed needles
1 pair size 6 U.S. (4 mm)
needles *or size to obtain gauge*
39 in. (1 m) ribbon, 3/8 in. (10 mm) wide
Stitch markers
Tapestry needle

GAUGE
28 sts and 36 rows = 4 in. (10 cm) in Stockinette St. (p. 124)

TO MAKE HAT
Using yarn (B) and larger dpns, cast on 70 sts and divide between three needles. Join into the round, taking care not to twist sts, and mark beginning of first round. Work in Stockinette St. until work measures 1 in. (2.5 cm). Change to yarn (A) and cont in Stockinette St. until work measures 4 in. (10 cm) from cast-on edge.

Crown
Next round *K2tog, k8; rep from * around.
Work 3 rounds in Stockinette St.
Next round *K2tog, k7; rep from * around.
Work 3 rounds in Stockinette St.
Next round *K2tog, k6; rep from * around.
Work 3 rounds in Stockinette St.
Next round *K2tog, k5; rep from * around.
Work 3 rounds in Stockinette St.—42 sts.
Next round *K2tog; rep from * around.
Break yarn. Thread a tapestry needle and run through rem sts. Pull tightly and secure. Securely weave in ends.

FINISHING
Flower (Make 1)
Using straight needles and yarn (B), cast on 35 sts.
Row 1 (WS) *K1, cast off 5 sts (2 sts on RH needle); rep from * to end—10 sts.
Run threaded tapestry needle through rem sts

continued on page 14

on needle. Pull tightly and secure.

Sew flower onto hat just above the brim.

Using yarn (A), work French knot (p. 121) in center of flower: Bring needle from back to front of work, wrap yarn around needle 10 times, use thumb to hold in place while pulling needle through wraps, then pass needle through to back of work in place where it emerged and fasten off.

Securely weave in ends.

TO MAKE SLIPPERS

Soles (Make 2)

Using yarn (A) and straight needles, cast on 9 sts. Work 1 row in Moss St. (p. 122)

Next row Cont in Moss St., inc 1 st at both ends by knitting into the front and back of first and last sts —11 sts.

Cont until work measures 3½ in. (9 cm).

Next row Dec 1 st at beg and end of next row.

Cast off rem 9 sts.

Uppers (Make 2)

Using yarn (A) and straight needles, cast on 19 sts. Work 1 row in Moss St.

Cont in Moss St., inc 1 st at end of next row, then at same edge on foll 5 rows—25 sts.

Work 4 more rows, finishing at straight edge.

Cast off 12 sts at start of next row. Work to end.

Dec 1 st at end of next row and beg of foll row—11 sts.

Work 1 row, casting on 1 st at end of row—12 sts.

Work 1 row.

Cast on 13 sts at end of next row—25 sts. Work 4 rows, then dec 1 st at toe end on next 6 rows. Cast off rem 19 sts.

FINISHING

Using tapestry needle, join seams with a slip stitch (p. 124) on WS. Seam straight edges on uppers to create back of heel. Insert sole. Turn to right side.

Using yarn (B), make 2 flowers as before. Attach one flower to each slipper at center front straight edge, working French knot with yarn (A) in center of flower as before.

Securely weave in ends.

TO MAKE MITTENS

Using yarn (A) and smaller dpns, cast on 27 sts and divide between three needles. Join into the round, taking care not to twist sts. Mark beginning of first round. Work 1¾ in. (4.5 cm) in Moss St. and then work eyelet round:

Next round K1, *k2tog, yo; rep from * around. Change to larger dpns and cont in Stockinette St. until work measures 4 in. (10 cm) from cast-on edge. Shorten or lengthen here if needed.

Shape Top of Mitten

Round 1 (K1, ssk, k8, k2tog) twice, k1.
Round 2 Knit.
Round 3 (K1, ssk, k6, k2tog) twice, k1.
Round 4 Knit.
Round 5 (K1, ssk, k4, k2tog) twice, k1.
Cast off.

FINISHING

Sew top seam of mitten on inside. Securely weave in ends. Thread ribbon through eyelets.

The slippers and mittens keep out the cold—and make baby stylish.

Baby Love Blanket

I've knit this blanket many times and in many colorways. I love the simplicity of the stripes and the amazement on the faces of parents when they suddenly see the hidden heart. This is a good project for practicing shadow knitting, as it is limited to the center square. The rest of the blanket knits up in a flash with good old garter stitch.

SKILL LEVEL
Intermediate

TIME TO KNIT
Long weekend

FINISHED MEASUREMENTS
32 in. (81 cm) square

YARN
Rowan Cashsoft DK
126 yd. (115 m) per 50 g ball:

Colorway 1 (p. 16)
5 balls Vamp 532 (A)
4 balls Dusty 542 (B)
1 ball Poppy 512 (C)

Colorway 2 (p. 19, left)
5 balls Navy 514 (A)
5 balls Cream 500 (B)
2 balls Poppy 512 (C)

Colorway 3 (p. 19, right)
From my stash
5 balls Turquoise (A)
5 balls Stone (B)
2 balls Dusty Rose (C)

NOTIONS
1 pair size 4 U.S. (3.5 mm) needles
1 pair size 6 U.S. (4 mm) needles *or size to obtain gauge*
Stitch markers
Tapestry needle

GAUGE
20 sts and 40 rows = 4 in. (10 cm) in Garter St. (p. 121)

Note
Slip the first stitch and knit into the back of the last stitch on every row to make selvage.

TO MAKE BLANKET
Using size 6 U.S. (4 mm) needles and yarn (A), cast on 149 sts.
Rows 1 and 2 Using yarn (A), work in Garter St.
Rows 3 and 4 Change to yarn (B). Continue working in Garter St.
Rep rows 1–4, ending on row 2, until work measures approximately 13 in. (33 cm) from cast-on edge.

Center Square
Work in Garter St. for 61 sts. Pm, then work 27 sts of the Center Square Chart. Place another stitch marker and cont in Garter St. for rem 61 sts—149 sts. Work 46 rows of the Center Square Chart, then cont in Garter St. for a further 13 in. (33 cm). Cast off in yarn (A).

continued on page 19

Center Square Chart

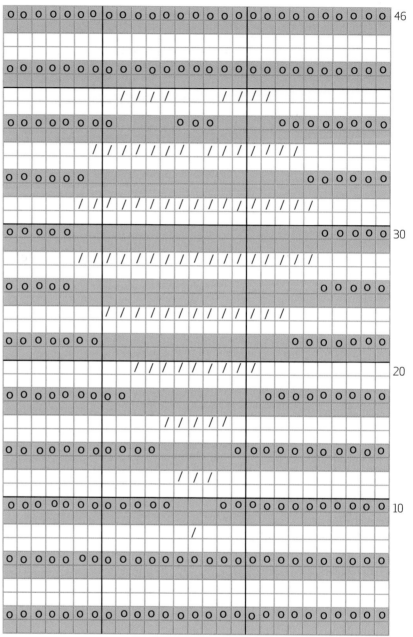

27

    Knit on RS, purl on WS using yarn (B)

 O Knit on WS (makes ridge on RS) using yarn (B)

    Knit on RS, purl on WS using yarn (C)

 / Knit on WS (makes ridge on RS) using yarn (C)

Baby Love Schematic

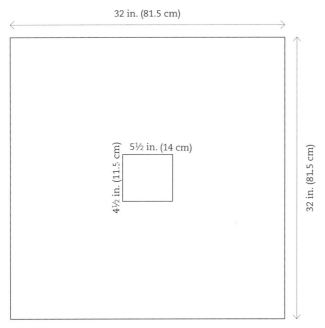

32 in. (81.5 cm)

5½ in. (14 cm)

4½ in. (11.5 cm)

32 in. (81.5 cm)

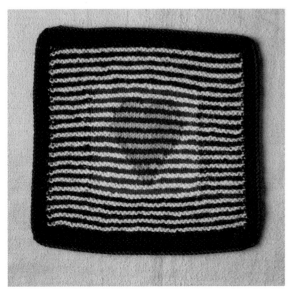

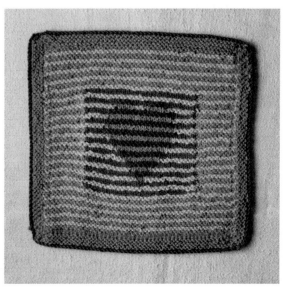

Swatches of the Navy and Turquoise blankets hide hearts of red and purple, respectively.

FINISHING
Block lightly on WS.

Edging
Using size 4 U.S. (3.5 mm) needles and yarn (A), pick up and knit 150 sts along one side of blanket.

Working in Garter St., knit 7 rows, inc 1 st after first and before last st at both ends of first and every other row. Using yarn (C), work 1 row, then cast off. Rep edging on the other three sides. Sew mitered edges of corners together neatly. Securely weave in all ends.

Whoopla Beanbags

I remember playing with beanbags when I started primary school—solid colors for different teams. For knitters not yet confident with intarsia, solid colors are also an option here. But I wanted to make this set more useful for the baby and toddler. On one side, they can learn to recognize numbers, and on the other side, practice counting with the corresponding apple, ducks, and hearts. If you're wondering about the name, it was invented by two of my granddaughters for a game where they throw soft toys high in the air.

SKILL LEVEL
Intermediate

TIME TO KNIT
Day

FINISHED MEASUREMENTS
5 in. (12.75 cm) square

YARN
Rowan Handknit Cotton
93 yd. (85 m) per 50 g ball:
1 ball each Rosso 215 (A), Florence 350 (B), Ecru 251 (C), Gooseberry 219 (D), Ochre 349 (E), Linen 205 (F), Thunder 335 (G), Atlantic 346 (H), Slick 313 (J), and Pacific 358 (K)

NOTIONS
1 pair size 6 U.S. (4 mm) needles *or size to obtain gauge*
Tapestry needle
Polystyrene beans

GAUGE
20 sts and 28 rows = 4 in. (10 cm) in Stockinette St. (p. 124)

Note
Leaving a long tail ensures that the final seam can be undone easily to wash the bag.

TO MAKE BEANBAGS
Using yarn (B), cast on 25 sts. Refer to Number One Chart and work the 34 rows in Stockinette St. Cast off. Using yarn (A), cast on 25 sts. Refer to Apple Chart and work the 34 rows in Stockinette St. Cast off. Using yarn (G), cast on 25 sts. Refer to Number Two Chart and work the 34 rows in Stockinette St. Cast off. Using yarn (D), cast on 25 sts. Refer to Ducks Chart and work the 34 rows in Stockinette St. Cast off. Using yarn (J), cast on 25 sts. Refer to Number Three Chart and work the 34 rows in Stockinette St. Cast off. Using yarn (H), cast on 25 sts. Refer to Hearts Chart and work the 34 rows in Stockinette St. Cast off.

FINISHING
Match up two squares per beanbag to make a total of three beanbags:
Number One and Apple Charts
Number Two and Ducks Charts
Number Three and Hearts Charts

With RSs together oversew around three sides and half of fourth side, leaving an opening. Turn right side out and fill with polystyrene beans, then oversew opening on outside. Leave a long tail of yarn, using the tapestry needle to hide the tail on the inside.

continued on page 22

Squishy and tactile beanbags encourage exploring, throwing, and catching, but also counting.

Beanbag Charts Key

- ■ Rosso 215 (A)
- ■ Florence 350 (B)
- □ Ecru 251 (C)
- ▨ Gooseberry 219 (D)
- ▨ Ochre 349 (E)
- ▨ Linen 205 (F)
- ■ Thunder 335 (G)
- ▨ Atlantic 346 (H)
- ■ Slick 313 (J)
- ■ Pacific 358 (K)

Number One Chart

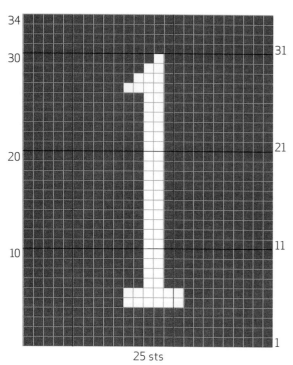

25 sts

Apple Chart

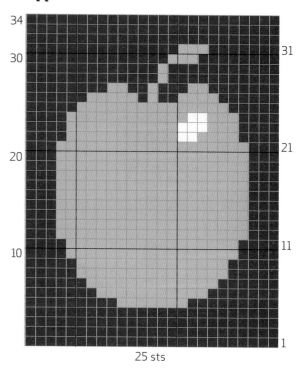

25 sts

Number Two Chart

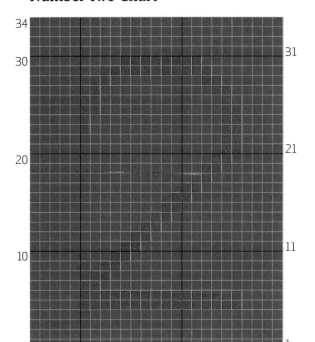

25 sts

Ducks Chart

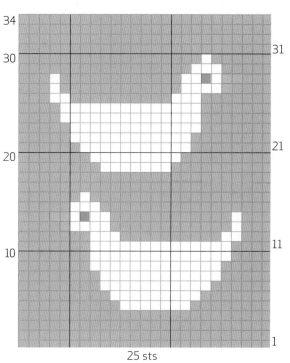

25 sts

Number Three Chart

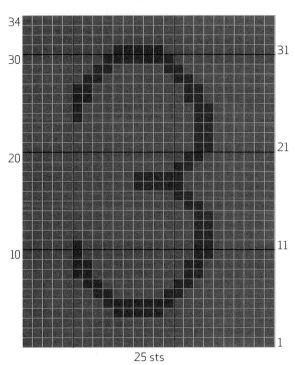

25 sts

Hearts Chart

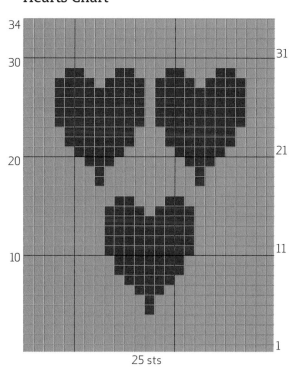

25 sts

Jubilee Jacket and Hat

This intricate toddler jacket with matching hat will be sure to endear you to the child's parents forever. Inspired by the Selbu knitting of Norway, I've used Baby Merino Silk DK for its fabulously soft and luxurious hand, but you can use any yarn. The tiny knots give a sculptured effect to the body and sleeves, and I've added mother-of-pearl heart-shaped buttons to echo the hearts in the Fair Isle pattern. It's an heirloom gift to treasure.

SKILL LEVEL
Advanced

TIME TO KNIT
Vacation

FINISHED MEASUREMENTS
Jacket
Small: To fit 2-year-old; 14 in. (35 cm)
long, 13 in. (34.5 cm) wide
Medium: To fit 3-year-old; 14 in. (37 cm)
long, 14 in. (37 cm) wide
Large: To fit 4-year-old; 15 in. (39.5 cm)
long, 16 in. (40.5 cm) wide

Hat
Small: 8 in. (20 cm) long, 16 in.
(40.5 cm) around brim
Medium: 8½ in. (21.5 cm) long, 17 in.
(44.5 cm) around brim
Large: 9 in. (23 cm) long, 18 in.
(45.7 cm) around brim

Note:
Pattern is written for size Small,
with Medium and Large instructions
in parentheses where necessary.

YARN
Rowan Baby Merino Silk DK
147 yd. (135 m) per 50 g ball:

5 (6, 6) balls Strawberry 687 (A)
3 (3, 4) balls Straw 671 (B)
1 (1, 1) ball Deep 682 (C)

NOTIONS
1 pair size 3 U.S. (3.25 mm) needles
1 pair size 6 U.S. (4 mm) needles *or size to obtain gauge*
Size G-6 (4 mm) crochet hook
Six ½-in. (13 mm) buttons
Stitch holders
Tapestry needle

GAUGE
24 sts and 28 rows = 4 in. (10 cm) in Knot pattern
24 sts and 24 rows = 4 in. (10 cm) in Fair Isle pattern

Note
Slip the first stitch and knit into the back of the last stitch on every row to make selvage. For more information on knitting Fair Isle, see p. 121.

TO MAKE JACKET
Back
Using smaller needles and yarn (A), cast on 79 (85, 95) sts and work 10 rows in Moss St. (p. 122), inc 1 st at end of final row—80 (86, 96) sts.
Change to larger needles. Refer to Jubilee Heart Chart and work rows 1–17, then rep rows 10–17 up to armhole, centering the chart as follows:
Row 1 Work last 4 (7, 0) sts of chart, work the 24 sts 3 (3, 4) times, work the first 4 (7, 0) sts.

continued on page 26

Jubilee Heart Chart

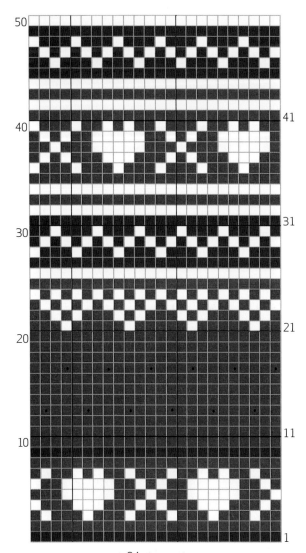

24 st repeat

- ▪ Work knot in (A)—p1, k1, p1, k1 into this st, making 4 sts from 1, then pass 2nd, 3rd, and 4th sts over first stitch.

- ▪ Strawberry 687 (A)
- ☐ Straw 671 (B)
- ▪ Deep 682 (C)

When work measures 8 (8¼, 8¾) in. [20.5 (21, 22) cm] from cast-on edge, ending on either a row 12 or row 16, shape armhole: Beginning on Jubilee Heart Chart row 21 and continuing to end, work rows 21–50. When chart is completed, rep rows 33 and 34, striping to end. **At the same time** cast off 4 (5, 6) sts at beg of next 2 rows. Then dec 1 st at both ends of next and every other row 5 (6, 9) times, keeping chart correct—62 (64, 66) sts. When work measures 13½ (14, 15) in. [34 (35.5, 38) cm] from cast-on edge, ending on WS row, shape neck:
Next row (RS) Work 18 (19, 19) sts, turn and leave rem sts on stitch holder.
Work each side of neck separately.
Next row Dec 1 st at beg of row.
Next row Cast off 8 sts at beg of row.
Next row Dec 1 st at beg of row.
Cast off rem 8 (9, 9) sts. With RS facing, place center 26 (26, 28) sts on stitch holder. Join yarn to rem sts and work to correspond to first side, reversing shaping.

Left Front
Using smaller needles and yarn (A), cast on 39 (43, 47) sts and work 10 rows in Moss St., increasing 1 (0, 1) st at end of final row—40 (43, 48) sts. Change to larger needles. Refer to Jubilee Heart Chart and work rows 1–17, then rep rows 10–17 up to armhole, centering the chart as follows:
Row 1 Work last 4 (7, 0) sts of chart, work the 24 sts 1 (1, 2) times, work the first 12 (12, 0) sts. When work measures 8 (8¼, 8¾) in. [20.5 (21, 22) cm] from cast-on, ending on either a row 12 or row 16, shape armhole:
Beginning on Jubilee Heart Chart row 21, work to row 50. When chart is completed, rep rows 33 and 34, striping to end.
At the same time cast off 4 (5, 6) sts at beg of next row. Work 1 row. Then dec 1 st at beg of next and every other row 5 (6, 9) times, keeping chart correct—31 (32, 33) sts. When work measures 11½ (12, 13) in. [29 (30.5, 33) cm] from cast-on edge, ending on RS row, shape neck:
Cast off 4 (4, 5) sts at beg of next row. Dec 1 neck edge st on next and every foll row 11 times,

Jubilee Jacket Schematic

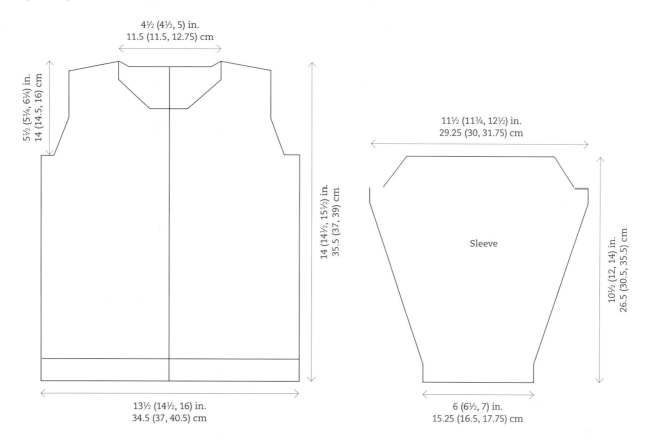

4½ (4½, 5) in.
11.5 (11.5, 12.75) cm

5½ (5¾, 6¼) in.
14 (14.5, 16) cm

14 (14½, 15½) in.
35.5 (37, 39) cm

13½ (14½, 16) in.
34.5 (37, 40.5) cm

11½ (11¾, 12½) in.
29.25 (30, 31.75) cm

Sleeve

10½ (12, 14) in.
26.5 (30.5, 35.5) cm

6 (6½, 7) in.
15.25 (16.5, 17.75) cm

keeping chart correct. Continue until work measures 13¾ (14¼, 15¼) in. [35 (36, 38.75) cm] from cast-on edge, then shape shoulder: Cast off 8 sts at beg of next row. Work 1 row. Cast off rem 8 (9, 9) sts.

Right Front
Work as for Left Front, reversing all shaping. Center chart as follows:
Row 1 Work last 12 (12, 0) sts of Jubilee Heart Chart, work 24 sts 1 (1, 2) times, work first 4 (7, 0) sts.

Sleeves
Using smaller needles and yarn (A), cast on 35 (37, 41) sts. Work 8 rows in Moss St., increasing 1 st in first st of final row—36 (38, 42) sts. Change to larger needles. Refer to Jubilee Heart Chart and work rows 1–17, then rep rows 10–17 to end, centering the chart as follows:

Row 1 Work last 6 (7, 9) sts of chart, work the 24 sts once, work the first 6 (7, 9) sts. **At the same time** inc 1 st at both ends of every other row 8 (5, 3) times, then every 4th row 8 (11, 14) times—68 (70, 76) sts. Continue until work measures 8½ (9½, 10½) in. [21.5 (24, 26.5) cm] from cast-on edge.

Shape top of sleeve
Cast off 4 (5, 6) sts at beg of next 2 rows. Then dec 1 st at both ends of next and every other row 5 (6, 9) times, keeping chart correct. Cast off the rem 50 (58, 46) sts.

FINISHING
Securely weave ends into like colors. Press lightly to size on inside. Sew shoulder seams. Set sleeves into armholes, joining side and sleeve seams in one line.

I used the two-handed Fair Isle method to help prevent puckering— it's easier than you might think.

Button Band

Using smaller needles and yarn (A), cast on 5 sts and work in Moss St., sewing band to Left Front (or Right Front for boy) and stretching slightly while knitting. Cont until band fits neck to shaping. Cast off. Place markers for six buttons on band, the first and last ¼ in. (0.5 cm) from outer edges, and the rem 4 spaced evenly between.

Buttonhole Band

Work as for button band, working buttonholes on RS rows opposite stitch markers as follows: Work 2, yo, k2tog, work final st.

Collar

Using smaller needles and yarn (A), with RS facing, beg 2 sts inside of Right Front band, pick up and knit 26 (26, 27) sts to shoulder seam, 3 sts down back neck, 26 (26, 28) sts from stitch holder at center back, 4 sts up along back neck, 26 (26, 27) sts along left neck edge, ending 2 sts in from center front edge—85 (85, 89) sts.

Row 1 (WS) *K1, p1; rep from * to last st, k1.
Row 2 *P1, k1; rep from * to last st, p1.
Rep last 2 rows once more, then cont as follows:
Row 1 (WS) K1, inc 1 st in next st, then starting with p1, work in Moss St. to last 2 sts, inc 1 st in next st, k1.
Row 2 P1, work in Moss St. to last st, p1.
Rep these 2 rows until collar measures 2 (2, 2¼) in. [5 (5, 5.75) cm] from start of Moss St. and then cast off all sts loosely in patt.

Sew buttons to Button Band, taking care that the pattern is in line across the jacket.

TO MAKE JESTER HAT
Front and Back (Make 2)

Using smaller needles and yarn (A), cast on 53 (56, 59) sts. Work 1 in. (2.5 cm) in k1, p1 rib, dec 1 st at end of final row on Small and Large sizes only— 52 (56, 58) sts.

Refer to Jubilee Heart Chart and work rows 1–17, then rep rows 10–17 to end, centering the chart as follows:

Work the last 2 (4, 5) sts of chart, work the 24 sts of chart twice, work the first 2 (4, 5) sts.

Cast off when work measures 8 (8½, 9) in. [20.5 (21.5, 23) cm] from cast-on edge, ending on WS row.

FINISHING

Using tapestry needle, sew on inside along side seams and cast-off edge, leaving ribbed edge open. Securely weave ends into like colors.

Tassels

Cut two 12-in. (30 cm) lengths of yarn each in (A), (B), and (C). Place all 6 lengths together. Put crochet hook through corner of top of hat, pull center of yarn through, and then put the ends of yarn through the loop created. Pull tightly. Repeat on opposite corner of hat. Trim tassels to even length.

CHAPTER 2

Hers

HERE YOU'LL FIND 11 VERSATILE AND WIDE-RANGING PROJECTS, from the glam and glorious frippery of the **Froufrou Gloves**, **Amulet Purse**, and **Glow Wristlets** to the cool and cozy **Zebra Mittens**, **Galaxy Beret**, and **Jive Leg Warmers**.

Shawls are a must-have, so there's the delicate **Will-o'-the-Wisp Shawlette** and the **Kitten's Paw Stole**, each in two different yarn weights. The **Deco Backpack** is a 1920s-inspired bag in a simple slip-stitch pattern—a great technique for adding color without tears. The collection is rounded off by the **Fiesta Shrug**, a basic lace pattern for beginners, which could also easily be transformed into a stole or scarf.

And there's a plethora of techniques to sink your teeth into, from lace, beaded knitting, and swirl knitting to cables, brioche, short rows, and slip-stitch knitting. Finishings include picot edging, fringes, I-cord, and single crochet. I had a great time choosing a collection of gifts I'd love to receive myself!

Fiesta Shrug and Fingerless Gloves

While swatching an alternative colorway for this shrug, I suddenly had a lightbulb moment—my swatch would make one fabulous pair of fingerless gloves. It's a win-win situation, in which the gloves perfectly illustrate the different hues while providing knitters with a way to use up spare yarn after making the shrug. Not a shrug sort of girl? Just omit the sewing up, put a frill down each long side, and you have a gorgeous stole. If you can't bear to give the shrug or stole away, you can gift the gloves instead— they are perfect for everyday wear or a glammed-up evening out.

~~~~~~

SKILL LEVEL
Beginner

TIME TO KNIT
Gloves
Weekend

Shrug
Vacation

FINISHED MEASUREMENTS
Gloves
3½ in. (9 cm) wide, 8 in. (20 cm) long

Shrug
Extra-Small: To fit bust 30–32 in.
(76–81 cm)
Small: To fit bust 34–36 in. (86–91 cm)
Medium: To fit bust 38–40 in. (96.5–102 cm)
Large: To fit bust 42–44 in. (107–112 cm)
Extra-Large: To fit bust 46–48 in.
(117–122 cm)
Extra-Extra-Large: To fit bust 50–52 in.
(127–132 cm)

Note
Pattern is written for size Extra-Small, with Small, Medium, Large, Extra-Large, and Extra-Extra-Large instructions in parentheses where necessary.

YARN
Rowan Panama
148 yd. (135 m) per 50 g ball:

Gloves
Red/Orange Colorway
1 ball each of Straw 313 (A), Begonia 306 (B),
Tulip 307 (C), Dahlia 305 (D), and Orchid 304 (E)
Blue/Green Colorway (shown at right)
1 ball each of Mizzle 314 (A), Aster 310 (B),
Cosmos 303 (C), Morning Glory 302 (D), and Lotus 309 (E)

Shrug
Red/Orange Colorway (shown on p. 35 and p. 37)
2 (2, 3, 3, 3, 4) balls Straw 313 (A)
2 (2, 3, 3, 3, 4) balls Begonia 306 (B)
2 (3, 3, 3, 4, 4) balls Tulip 307 (C)
2 (3, 3, 3, 4, 4) balls Dahlia 305 (D)
2 (2, 3, 3, 3, 4) balls Orchid 304 (E)
Blue/Green Colorway
2 (2, 3, 3, 3, 4) balls Mizzle 314 (A)
2 (2, 3, 3, 3, 4) balls Aster 310 (B)
2 (3, 3, 3, 4, 4) balls Cosmos 303 (C)
2 (3, 3, 3, 4, 4) balls Morning Glory 302 (D)
2 (2, 3, 3, 3, 4) balls Lotus 309 (E)

NOTIONS
1 pair size 2 U.S. (2.75 mm) needles
1 pair size 3 U.S. (3.25 mm) needles

continued on page 34

Fiesta Fingerless Gloves Schematic

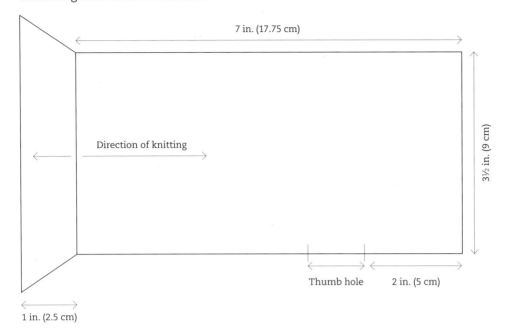

7 in. (17.75 cm)

Direction of knitting

3½ in. (9 cm)

Thumb hole   2 in. (5 cm)

1 in. (2.5 cm)

Size 3 U.S. (3.25 mm) 29-in. or 32-in. circular needle *or size to obtain gauge*
Size D-3 (3.25 mm) crochet hook
Stitch markers
Tapestry needle

GAUGE
26 sts and 40 rows = 4 in. (10 cm) in Old Shale pattern when blocked

TO MAKE GLOVES (MAKE 2)
Using yarn (A) and larger needles, cast on 42 sts. Begin Old Shale pattern (multiple of 6 sts), rep the 4-row color sequence as foll:
Row 1 (RS) Knit.
Row 2 Purl.
Row 3 *K2 tog, (yo, k1) twice, k2 tog; rep from *.
Row 4 Knit.
Rep rows 1–4 using yarn (B).
Rep rows 1–4 using yarn (C).
Rep rows 1–4 using yarn (D).
Rep rows 1–4 using yarn (E).
Rep rows 1–4 using yarn (D).
Rep rows 1–4 using yarn (C).
Rep rows 1–4 using yarn (B).

Rep the 32-row sequence twice, then work 4 rows in yarn (A)—68 rows.
Change to smaller needles and yarn (A).
Work 2 rows in Garter St. (p. 121), then cast off.

FINISHING
With RS facing, use larger straight needles and yarn (B) to pick up and knit 42 sts evenly along cast-on edge.

Frill
Row 1 (WS) Using yarn (B), knit to form ridge on RS.
Rows 2 and 4 Using yarn (B), knit.
Rows 3 and 5 Using yarn (B), purl.
Row 6 Change to yarn (A) and knit into front, back, and front again of every st—126 sts.
Row 7 Using yarn (A), purl.
Row 8 Using yarn (E), knit.
Using yarn (E), cast off purlwise.
Use a small neat backstitch on edge of work to firm seam.
Join side seam, leaving 1-in. (2.5 cm) gap for thumb starting 3 in. (7.5 cm) from top of glove. Using yarn (E) and crochet hook, work 1 row of sc (p. 123) to neaten thumb hole. Securely weave in all ends.

The simple 4-row pattern creates lacy colorful waves, finished with a frill to echo the undulating movement.

TO MAKE SHRUG

Using larger straight needles and yarn (A), cast on 86 (98, 110, 122, 134, 146) sts and work in Old Shale pattern:

Row 1 (RS) Sl 1, knit to last st, k1tbl.

Row 2 Sl 1, purl to last st, k1tbl.

Row 3 Sl 1, *(k2 tog) twice, (yo, k1) 4 times, (k2tog) twice; rep from * to last st, k1tbl.

Row 4 Sl 1, knit to last st, k1tbl.

Rep rows 1–4 using yarn (B).

Rep rows 1–4 using yarn (C).

Rep rows 1–4 using yarn (D).

Rep rows 1–4 using yarn (E).

Rep rows 1–4 using yarn (D).

Rep rows 1–4 using yarn (C).

Rep rows 1–4 using yarn (B).

continued on page 36

Fiesta Shrug Schematic

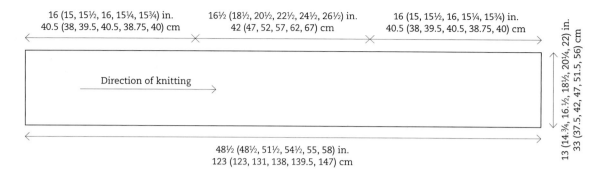

16 (15, 15½, 16, 15¼, 15¾) in.
40.5 (38, 39.5, 40.5, 38.75, 40) cm

16½ (18½, 20½, 22½, 24½, 26½) in.
42 (47, 52, 57, 62, 67) cm

16 (15, 15½, 16, 15¼, 15¾) in.
40.5 (38, 39.5, 40.5, 38.75, 40) cm

Direction of knitting

13 (14.¾, 16.½, 18½, 20¼, 22) in.
33 (37.5, 42, 47, 51.5, 56) cm

48½ (48½, 51½, 54½, 55, 58) in.
123 (123, 131, 138, 139.5, 147) cm

Rep the 32-row sequence 15 (15, 16, 17, 17 18) times. Work 4 rows in yarn (A), then cast off— 484 (484, 516, 548, 548, 580) rows.

FINISHING
Securely weave ends into like colors.

Cuff Frill
Using larger straight needles and yarn (B) and with RS facing, pick up and knit 50 (50, 50, 56, 56, 56) sts evenly along cuff edge.
Row 1 (WS), for cast-on edge
Using yarn (B), knit, to form ridge on RS.
Row 1 (WS), for cast-off edge using yarn (B) Purl, to form ridge on RS.
Row 2 Knit.
Row 3 Purl.
Row 4 Knit.
Row 5 Purl.
Row 6 Change to yarn (A) and knit into front, back, and front again of every stitch— 150 (150, 150, 156, 156, 156) sts.
Row 7 Purl.
Row 8 Change to yarn (E). Knit.
Cast off purlwise.
Sew sleeve seams to underarm, sewing sides

of frill plus 16 (15, 15½, 16, 15¼, 15¾) in. [40.5 (38, 39, 40.5, 38.75, 40) cm] at beginning and end of work, leaving the center 16½ (18½, 20½, 22½, 24½, 26½) in. [42 (47, 52, 57, 62, 67) cm] unseamed.

Body Frill
Divide the unseamed side edges of shrug into 8 equal parts and mark with stitch markers. Using circular needle and yarn (B), with RS facing, pick up and knit 27 (30, 33, 37, 40, 43) sts in each section—216 (240, 264, 296, 320, 344) sts.
Next row Purl.
Work rows 2–8 as for cuff frill, following pattern and color sequence, purling row 1.
Block to size. Securely weave ends into like colors.

Jive Leg Warmers

These chunky leg warmers are ideal for getting you *au courant* with basic cables.
Knit flat with no shaping, this is a gift you can knit up on a long winter's evening
or over a leisurely weekend. I'm so happy leg warmers are back in fashion:
Whether they're worn on stage, on the street, or at home, they certainly help
bring out the dancer in everyone.

SKILL LEVEL
Intermediate

TIME TO KNIT
Day

FINISHED MEASUREMENTS
10 in. (25 cm) around, 13 in. (33 cm) long

YARN
Rowan Big Wool
87 yd. (80 m) per 100 g ball:

Green Leg Warmers
2 balls Reseda 069

Purple Leg Warmers
2 balls Wild Berry 025

NOTIONS
1 pair size U.S. 13 (9 mm) needles
1 pair size U.S. 17 (12 mm) needles
or size to obtain gauge
Cable needle
Tapestry needle

GAUGE
13 sts and 13 rows = 4 in. (10 cm) in
cable pattern

TO MAKE LEG WARMERS (MAKE 2)
Using smaller needles, cast on 32 sts
and work 8 rows in k1, p1 rib.
Change to larger needles and begin
cable pattern (multiple of 8 sts).
Row 1 (RS) Sl 1, knit to last st, k1tbl.
Row 2 Sl 1, purl to last st, k1tbl.
Row 3 *Sl next 2 sts onto cn and hold at front
of work, k2, k2 from cn, k4; rep from * to last st, k1tbl.
Row 4 Sl 1, purl to last st, k1tbl.
Row 5 Sl 1, knit to last st, k1tbl.
Row 6 Sl 1, purl to last st, k1tbl.
Row 7 *K4, sl next 2 sts to cn and hold at back
of work, k2, k2 from cn; rep from * to last st, k1tbl.
Row 8 Sl 1, purl to last st, k1tbl.
Rep these 8 rows 4 times. Work should measure
12 in. (30.5 cm) from the cast-on edge.
Change to smaller needles and work 4 rows
more in k1, p1 rib.
Cast off loosely in rib.

FINISHING
Using tapestry needle, sew side seam on
WS edge of work. Securely weave in all ends.

Glow Wristlets

Dress these wristlets up or down, depending on the occasion. Whether they're keeping your wrists warm while you're typing on the computer, or worn as an accent when you're decked out for a party, these wristlets rock. To spice up a boring business outfit, try black with silver beads or white with black beads. You can also get creative with the color by striping the background in toning or contrasting hues. No matter what you choose, it's a great little last-minute gift to knit.

SKILL LEVEL
Beginner

TIME TO KNIT
Day

FINISHED MEASUREMENTS
3¾ in. (9.5 cm) long, 6 in. (16.5 cm) wide

YARN
Rowan Wool Cotton
123 yd. (113 m) per 50 g ball:

Purple Wristlet
1 ball Flower 943

Blue Wristlet
1 ball Pier 983

NOTIONS
1 pair size 3 U.S. (3.25 mm) needles
1 pair size 5 U.S. (3.75 mm) needles
or size to obtain gauge
1 pack Debbie Abrahams size 6 black beads (Purple Wristlet)
1 pack Debbie Abrahams size 6 silver beads (Blue Wristlet)
Fine sewing needle or Big Eye needle
Tapestry needle

GAUGE
24 sts and 32 rows = 4 in. (10 cm) in Stockinette Stitch (p. 124)

SPECIAL ABBREVIATION
Bead 1
Bring yarn to RS of work, slide bead up to the st just worked, slip next st purlwise, and bring yarn to WS of work, leaving bead on RS in front of the slipped st.

TO MAKE WRISTLETS (MAKE 2)
Thread 160 beads onto ball of Flower for Purple Wristlet or 184 beads onto ball of Pier for Blue Wristlet. Using smaller needles, cast on 40 sts and work 2 rows in Garter St. (p. 121). Change to larger needles. Refer to Purple Glow Chart or Blue Glow Chart and work the 28 rows, rep the 10 sts 4 times across row. Change to smaller needles and work 2 more rows in Garter St. Cast off loosely.

FINISHING
Oversew side edges of wristlets together on inside. Press lightly on the WS.

Purple Glow Chart

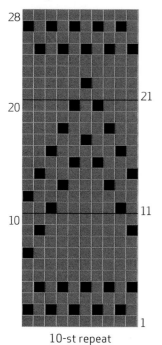

10-st repeat

Blue Glow Chart

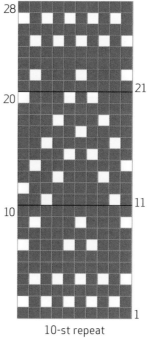

10-st repeat

■ Stockinette st in Flower 943
■ Place black bead on this stitch

■ Stockinette st in Pier 983
□ Place silver bead on this stitch

Froufrou Fingerless Gloves

These frothy concoctions in luxurious medium-weight yarn are a beautiful gift for a bride in white, ivory, or "something blue," as in the old rhyme. They'll also leave a non-knitting recipient completely in awe of your skills. Rest assured, though, this is an easy lace rib that knits up quickly, leaving you plenty of time to knit an extra pair for yourself.

SKILL LEVEL
Intermediate

TIME TO KNIT
Weekend

FINISHED MEASUREMENTS
Small: 3 in. (7.5 cm) wide, 8½ in. (21.5 cm) long
Medium: 3½ in. (9 cm) wide, 8½ in. (21.5 cm) long
Large: 4 in. (10 cm) wide, 8½ in. (21.5 cm) long

Note
Pattern is written for size Small, with Medium and Large instructions in parentheses where necessary.

YARN
Rowan Kidsilk Haze
229 yd. (210m) per 25g ball:

Pink Gloves (shown on p. 44)
1 (2, 2) balls Blushes 583

Turquoise Gloves
1 (2, 2) balls Trance 666

NOTIONS
1 pair size 5 U.S. (3.75 mm) needles
1 pair size 6 U.S. (4 mm) needles, plus 1 extra size 6 U.S. (4 mm) needle *or size to obtain gauge*
Stitch holders
Tapestry needle

GAUGE
27 sts and 36 rows = 4 in. (10 cm) in Lacy Rib pattern

SPECIAL ABBREVIATION
Lacy Rib
Row 1 *Sl 1 purlwise, k2, psso, k3. Rep from * to end.
Row 2 *P4, yo, p1. Rep from * to end.
Row 3 *K3, sl 1 purlwise, k2, psso. Rep from * to end.
Row 4 *P1, yo, p4. Rep from * to end.

continued on page 44

These lacy rib gloves are a good starter lace pattern with an easy 4-row repeat.

TO MAKE GLOVES (MAKE 2)

Frill 1

Using larger needles, cast on 122 (140, 158) sts loosely using the Lace Cast-On (p. 122). Work Lacy Rib for next 8 rows, slipping the first st and knitting into the back of the last st on every row.

Row 9 K1, *k3tog; rep from * to last st, k1—42 (48, 54) sts.

Change to smaller needles. Work 8 rows in k1, p1 rib. Place sts on holder.

Frill 2

Rep first 9 rows of Frill 1. Place Frill 2 on top of Frill 1 and, using the 3rd needle, work a WS row of Lacy

Froufrou Schematic

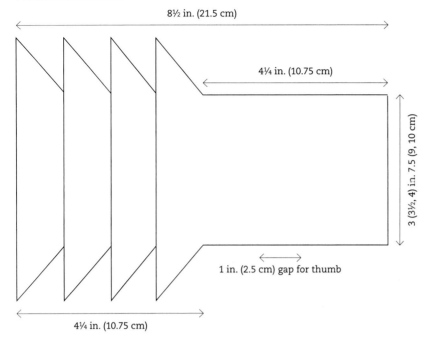

8½ in. (21.5 cm)

4¼ in. (10.75 cm)

3 (3½, 4) in. 7.5 (9, 10 cm)

1 in. (2.5 cm) gap for thumb

4¼ in. (10.75 cm)

Rib, holding front and back needles together
on the next row—2 frills attached, 42 (48, 54) sts.

Frill 3

*Change to smaller needles and cont on these
42 (48, 54) sts for a further 7 rows in k1, p1 rib.
Place sts on holder.
Rep first 9 rows of Frill 1, placing Frill 3 on top
of Frill 2 on RS. Join together in rib on WS row as
before using 3 needles **—3 frills attached,
42 (48, 54) sts.

Frill 4

Rep from * to ** as for Frill 3, joining Frill 4
on top of Frill 3—4 frills attached, 42 (48, 54) sts.
Cont on larger needles. Starting on row 1, cont in
Lacy Rib pattern for 3¾ in. (9.5 cm), ending on WS
row. Change to smaller needles and work 4 rows of
k1, p1 rib. Cast off using Lace Cast-Off (p. 122).

FINISHING

Backstitch (p. 118) along edge of work.
Join side seam (Lacy Rib and k1, p1 rib), leaving
1-in. (2.5 cm) gap for thumb starting 3 in. (7.5 cm)
from top of glove and ending 2 in. from top of
glove. Join each frill at side seam. Using the
tapestry needle, securely weave in all ends.

Amulet Purse

You can always rely on a beaded purse for the wow factor. Make the smaller version as a gift to send congratulations or get-well wishes. The larger purse is just the right size to hold the few bits and bobs we can't do without on celebration days.

SKILL LEVEL
Intermediate

TIME TO KNIT
Vacation

FINISHED MEASUREMENTS
Small: 2¼ in. (5.75 cm) wide, 3 in. (7.75 cm) deep (without tassels)
Large: 4½ in. (11.5 cm) wide, 5½ in. (14 cm) deep (without tassels)

YARN
Rowan Panama
148 yd. (135 m) per 50 g ball:
Small: 1 (2) balls Mizzle 314
Large: 1 (2) balls Aster 310

NOTIONS
Set of 4 size 2 U.S. (2.75 mm) double-pointed needles
Set of 4 size 3 U.S. (3.25 mm) double-pointed needles *or size to obtain gauge*
Size C-2 U.S. (3 mm) crochet hook
Stitch markers
Tapestry needle
Velcro® for closure (optional)
Beads (I used Debbie Abrahams)
For size Small:
1 pack of 500 size 8 pewter beads
1 pack of 500 size 8 aqua beads

For size Large:
Version 1
2 packs of 500 size 8 metallic silver beads
Version 2
2 packs of 500 size 8 metallic copper beads
Beading needle (I recommend a Big Eye needle)
Fine sewing needle and thread

GAUGE
27 sts and 36 rows = 4 in. (10 cm) in Stockinette Stitch (p. 124)

SPECIAL ABBREVIATION
Bead 1
Bring yarn to RS of work, slide bead up to the st just worked, slip next st purlwise, and take yarn to WS of work, leaving bead on RS in front of the slipped st.

Note
Thread beads onto each ball before starting to knit.
Here is the method using a beading needle instead of a Big Eye needle, which must be used when making the tassels for the fringe. Before using, check that the beading needle will go through the beads. Cut a length of thread about 6 in. (15 cm) long and thread both ends through the needle, thus forming a loop at one end. Pass one end of the yarn through the loop of the sewing thread. Hold the end of the yarn in place and slip the beads down the needle, along the thread, and over the doubled yarn.

continued on page 48

TO MAKE LARGE AMULET

Thread 480 beads onto yarn. Using larger dpns, cast on 60 sts, then distribute evenly onto 3 needles. Check that the cast-on edge is not twisted before joining into the round and pm at beginning of round.

Version 1 (shown on p. 46, left)

Work 50 rounds of the Large Amulet Version 1 Chart, working the 4 sts of the chart 15 times around.

Note

Row gauge on beaded knitting sometimes varies, and although your stitch gauge may be correct, the row gauge may be more difficult to achieve. If your row gauge is inaccurate at row 46, just rep rows 45 and 46 until the correct length is achieved, then cont with rows 47–50.

Work a final row on smaller needles and then cast off in Picot Point Cast-Off (p. 123).

Version 2 (shown on p. 46, right)

Refer to Large Amulet Version 2 Chart and work rows 1–10, rep the 4 sts of chart 15 times across row. Then rep rows 9 and 10 fifteen times more, working the final 10 rows as for Version 1.

To Make Short Strap

Thread 45 beads onto yarn. Using smaller needles, cast on 91 sts and work 3 rows as follows:

Row 1 Knit.
Row 2 Knit and place bead every other st.
Row 3 Cast off knitwise. Strap should measure 15 in. (38 cm) long.

To Make Long Strap

Thread 151 beads onto yarn. Using smaller needles, cast on 303 sts and work 5 rows as follows:

Rows 1 and 2 Knit.
Row 3 Purl and place bead every other st.
Row 4 Purl tbl.
Row 5 Cast off knitwise. Strap should measure 50 in. (127 cm) long.

FINISHING

Beaded Fringe

Cut 30 pieces of yarn 8 in. (20 cm) long for tassels. You will have to cut the sewing thread after every tassel when placing the beads on the doubled yarn, so leave a longer tail than usual (about 7 in. when doubled).

Thread yarn through the sewing thread loop so that you have a 4 in. (10 cm) tail of 2 strands. Knot the doubled yarn 1½ in. (3.75 cm) down from top of loop, then slide 3 beads into place above it. Use crochet hook to pull the loop of tassel through two thicknesses of cast-on st, then slip the open end through the loop. Pull tightly and rep across cast-on edge. When all tassels are in place, cut across bottom edge 1 in. (2.5 cm) below knot to neaten.

Attach straps and secure at inside top edges.

If desired, sew a thin strip of hook-and-loop tape to inside at top edge for a more secure closure.

TO MAKE SMALL AMULET (shown on p. 46, center)

Thread 50 beads onto knitting in the following order:

27 pewter
1 aqua
6 pewter
1 aqua
15 pewter

Rep this order twice more, then thread 12 more pewter beads—162 beads.

Using larger dpns, cast on 34 sts. Distribute sts evenly onto 3 needles, making sure the cast-on edge is not twisted before you join into the round. Place marker at beginning of round. Work the 27 rounds of the Small Amulet Chart, working the 17 sts twice around.

Using smaller dpns, cast off in Picot Point Cast-Off (p. 123).

FINISHING

Beaded Fringe

Make fringe as for Large Amulet with 1 tassel on every cast-on edge st, using 1 strand of yarn

Small Amulet Chart

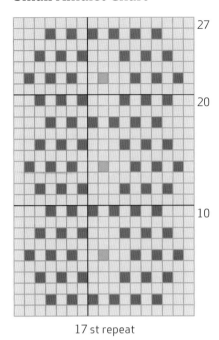

27

20

10

17 st repeat

- ⬛ Bead 1 using aqua
- ⬛ Bead 1 using pewter
- ⬜ Knit

Large Amulet
Version 1 Chart

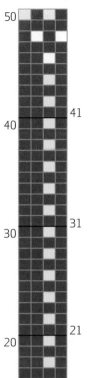

50

41

40

31

30

21

20

11

10

1

4 st
repeat

- ⬜ Bead 1
- ⬛ Knit

Large Amulet
Version 2 Chart

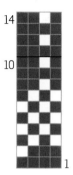

14

10

1

Amulet Schematic

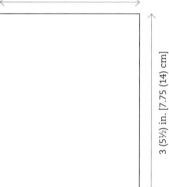

2¼ in. (4½) in. [5.75 (11.5) cm]

3 (5½) in. [7.75 (14) cm]

doubled for each tassel—17 tassels. Each tassel should have 3 beads threaded in the order of pewter, aqua, pewter.

Starting with the middle tassel, knot the doubled yarn 2¼ in. (5.75 cm) down from top of loop, then slide 3 beads as above into place above it. Subsequent tassels on both sides should be knotted 1 bead's depth above the last so that the beads form a chevron. Beads on the last 3 tassels on each side should all be level.

If required, sew a thin strip of hook-and-loop tape to inside at top edge.

Strap

Thread 130 aqua beads onto yarn. Using crochet hook, attach yarn at side seam and make a chain, incorporating 1 bead after every stitch until all 130 beads are used. Attach to opposite side seam and fasten off.

Deco Backpack

Color without complication in this two-tone pattern. Worked in a simple slip stitch using one color at a time, there's no carrying the yarn behind your work. Finished with a tie fastening or a wide garter band that frills when tied, this backpack will hold everything you need.

SKILL LEVEL
Intermediate

TIME TO KNIT
Weekend

FINISHED MEASUREMENTS
15 in. (38 cm) wide, 12 in. (30.5 cm) high, plus 3-in. (7.5 cm) band

YARN
Rowan Savannah
87 yd. (80 m) per 50 g ball:

Green with Purple Contrast Backpack (Version 1)
3 balls Prairie 932 (A)
5 balls Drifter 939 (B)

Blue with Green Contrast Backpack (Version 2)
3 balls Drifter 939 (A)
5 balls Grassland 935 (B)

NOTIONS
2 size 5 U.S. (3.75 mm) double-pointed needles
1 pair size 6 U.S. (4 mm) needles
Size 6 U.S. (4 mm) 24-in. circular needle
1 pair size 8 U.S. (5 mm) needles *or size to obtain gauge*
Size G-6 U.S. (4 mm) crochet hook
Stitch holders
2 yd. (2 m) Petersham ribbon, 1 in. (2.5 cm) wide
Tapestry needle

GAUGE
21 sts and 38 rows = 4 in. (10 cm) in pattern

Notes
Slip the first stitch and knit into the back of the last stitch on every row to make selvage. Slipped stitches are slipped purlwise. Always carry the yarn on WS when slipping stitches. If necessary, the yarn is brought forward or taken back before the next stitch.
For information on Color Slip Stitch Knitting, see p. 120

TO MAKE BACKPACK
Back and Front (Make 2)
Using size 8 U.S. (5 mm) needles and yarn (A), cast on 80 sts.
Foundation row Using yarn (A), sl 1, purl to last st, k1tbl.
Row 1 (RS) Using yarn (A), sl 1, knit to last st, k1tbl.
Row 2 Using yarn (A), sl 1, k6, *sl 2, k6; rep from * to last st, k1tbl.
Rows 3 and 4 Using yarn (A), rep row 2.
Row 5 Using yarn (B), sl 1, k6, *sl 2, k6; rep from * to last st, k1tbl.

continued on page 52

Row 6 Using yarn (B), sl 1, p6, *sl 2, p6; rep from * to last st, k1tbl.
Row 7 Using yarn (B), rep row 5.
Row 8 Using yarn (B), rep row 6.
Row 9 Using yarn (A), sl 1, knit to last st, k1tbl.
Row 10 Using yarn (A), sl 1, k2, sl 2, *k6, sl 2; rep from * to last 3 sts, k2, k1tbl.
Rows 11 and 12 Using yarn (A), rep row 10.
Row 13 Using yarn (B), sl 1, k2, sl 2, *k6, sl 2, rep from * to last 3 sts, k2, k1tbl.
Row 14 Using yarn (B), sl 1, p2, sl 2, *p6, sl 2, rep from * to last 3 sts, p2, k1tbl.
Row 15 Using yarn (B), rep row 13.
Row 16 Using yarn (B), rep row 14.
Rep these 16 rows 7 times, then work rows 1–4—116 rows. Place sts on holder.

FINISHING

Top of Backpack

With RS facing, change to yarn (B) and size 6 U.S. (4 mm) circular needle. Starting at center front, knit 40 sts from center to edge from holder, knit across the 80 sts on holder for back, then knit 40 sts from edge to front for center—160 sts. Knitting back and forth, work another 11 (13 for Version 2) rows in Garter St. (p. 121). Turn the backpack inside out and with WS facing, work casing across row:

Next row (RS) Place RH needle in front of first st as if to knit, then put needle through first loop on first row of Garter St. and knit together with the st above on LH needle. Rep this across row, forming a casing on RS.

Note

Some knitters may find it easier to work the casing if the stitches from the first row are placed on a smaller needle before the casing is worked, and thus the stitches can be knitted together from the two needles (see illustration at right).

Version 1

Turn the work back to the RS and continue in the round in Garter St. for 16 more rows. Then change to Stockinette St. for facing and work until facing is long enough to slip stitch in place over first row of Garter St. on inside.

Finishing the Top of the Bag

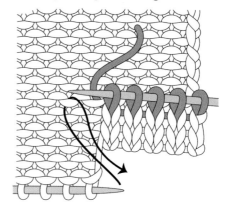

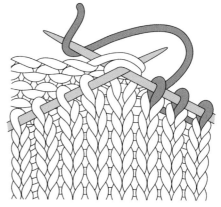

Version 2

Cast off with WS facing on inside.

Tie (Both versions)

Using 2 size 5 U.S. (3.75 mm) dpns and yarn (B), work I-Cord (p. 122) until work measures 42 in. (107 cm).
Thread tie through casing, beginning and ending at center front, then knot the ends of the tie.

Straps (Make 2)

Using size 6 U.S. (4 mm) needles and yarn (B), cast on 13 sts.
Row 1 (RS) Knit.
Row 2 P7, k6.
Rep these 2 rows until work measures 25 in. (63.5 cm) when stretched slightly.
Place 6 Garter Sts. on one st holder and 7 Stockinette Sts. on another. Fold lengthwise along center line and insert 25 in. (63.5 cm) of ribbon. Overstitch seam along long side.

Deco Backpack Version 1 Schematic

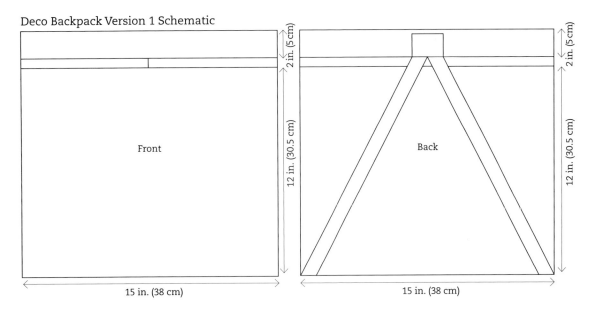

Deco Backpack Version 2 Schematic

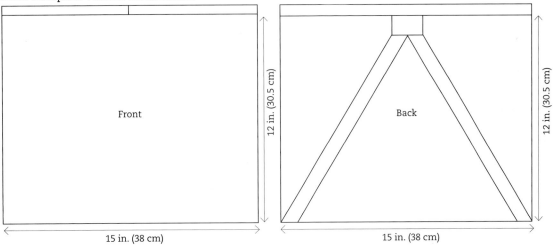

Note

If required, put a stitch in every few inches to hold the ribbon in place along the length of the straps.

Oversew cast-on edge.
Using size 6 U.S. (4 mm) needles and yarn (B), with Garter St. side of first strap facing, pick up and knit 1 st of Stockinette St., then *knit together 1 Garter St. and 1 Stockinette St.; rep 6 times. With Garter St. side of second strap facing, rep from * 6 times. Pick up and knit final st of Stockinette St.—14 sts.
Work 12 rows of Garter St. as foll:
Row 1 Sl 1, k12, k1tbl.
Rep this row.

Neatly slip stitch (p. 124) top of straps (side edges and top of last 12 rows of Garter St.) to center back on RS. Slip stitch on the band directly above the casing for Version 1. Slip stitch on the band directly below the casing for Version 2.
Oversew the other end of each strap on outside along bottom edge of back of backpack, each one starting in the corner.
Press to size on inside. Join side seams and seam along bottom of backpack with a small backstitch (p. 118). Securely weave ends into like colors.

Will-o'-the-Wisp Shawlette

This edge-to-edge short-row shawlette comes in two versions. The first calls for Fine Lace yarn with medium-weight yarn as a contrast and is bedecked with beads and adorned with crocheted edging. The other is simpler, with no finishing. The medium-weight yarn contrasts with the pure silk from my stash. Dig into your own stash and experiment with different yarns for more emphatic textured contrasts. Both use two different-sized needles to get a no-effort lacy effect.

SKILL LEVEL
Advanced

TIME TO KNIT
Vacation

FINISHED MEASUREMENTS
60 in. (152.5 cm) wide at top edge, 15 in. (38 cm) long

YARN
Pink and Purple Shawlette
(Version 1 shown at left)
Rowan Fine Lace
437 yd. (400 m) per 50 g ball:
1 ball Jewel 936 (A)
Rowan Kidsilk Haze
229 yd. (210 m) per 25 g ball:
1 ball Blushes 583 (B)
1 ball Burgundy (C)
(Note: This yarn is from my stash and the color is discontinued, but you could substitute with Liqueur 595.)

Green and Cream Shawlette
(Version 2 shown on p. 57)
Rowan Kidsilk Haze
229 yd. (210 m) per 25 g ball:
2 balls Jelly 597 (A)
1 ball Cream 634 (B)

Note
I used pure silk from my stash, which is thicker, for more texture.

NOTIONS
1 each of size 3 U.S. (3.25 mm) and size 10 U.S. (6 mm) needles, used as a pair *or size to obtain gauge*
1 pair size 4 U.S. (3.5 mm) needles
Size G-6 U.S. (4 mm) crochet hook (Version 1)
1 pack Debbie Abrahams size 8 #56 beads (Version 1)
Stitch markers

GAUGE
20 sts and 28 rows = 4 in. (10 cm) in Garter Stitch (p. 121) when blocked

TO MAKE SHAWLETTE
Using yarn (A) and size 10 U.S. (6 mm) needle, cast on 3 sts. Work in Garter St., alternating rows with the two different-sized needles. At the same time, inc 1 st at beg of 2nd and then every 4th row until 32 rows have been worked—11 sts.
Next row (RS) Using yarn (B) [(C) for Version 1], knit across all sts.
Begin short rows:
Rows 1 and 2 P2, wrap and turn, k1, m1 in next st.
Rows 3 and 4 P4, picking up the previous wrap when you come to it, wrap and turn, k3, m1 in next st.

continued on page 56

A mixture of yarn weights can work well together, as it does here for Version 1.

Rows 5 and 6 P6, picking up the previous wrap when you come to it, wrap and turn, k5, m1 in next st.

Rows 7 and 8 P8, picking up the previous wrap when you come to it, wrap and turn, k7, m1 in next st.

Row 9 Knit across row—15 sts.

*Change to yarn (A) and continue with increases as before at end of 3rd row, then every 4th row for 32 rows more** —23 sts.

Next row (RS) Using yarn (B), knit across all sts. Begin short rows, picking up the wraps on each WS row as you come to them as before:

Rows 1–8 Rep rows 1–8 as above.

Rows 9 and 10 P10, wrap and turn, k9, m1 in next st.

Row 11 Knit across row—28 sts. Using (A), rep from * to **—36 sts.

Next row (RS) Using (B) [(C) for Version 1], knit across all sts. Begin short rows, picking up the wraps on each WS row as you come to them as before:

Rows 1–10 Rep rows 1–10 as above.

Rows 11 and 12 P12, wrap and turn, k11, m1 in next st.

Row 13 Knit across all sts—42 sts. Using yarn (A), rep from * to **—50 sts.

Next row (RS) Using yarn (B), knit across all sts. Begin short rows, picking up the wraps on each WS row as you come to them as before:

Rows 1–12 Rep rows 1–12 as above.

Rows 13 and 14 P14, wrap and turn, k13, m1 in next st.

Row 15 Knit across all sts—57 sts. Using yarn (A), rep from * to **—65 sts.

Next row (RS) Using (B) [(C) for Version 1], knit across all sts. Begin short rows, picking up the wraps on each WS row as you come to them as before:

Rows 1–14 Rep rows 1–14 as above.

Rows 15 and 16 P16, wrap and turn, k15, m1 in next st.

Row 17 Knit across all sts—73 sts. Using yarn (A), rep from * to **—81 sts.

Center Triangle

Using size 4 U.S. (3.5 mm) needles and yarn (B), knit across all sts. Begin short rows:

Rows 1 and 2 Using yarn (B), p6, wrap and turn, k6.

Rows 3 and 4 Using yarn (C), [(A) for Version 2] p12, picking up the wrap when you come to it, wrap and turn, k12.

Rows 5 and 6 Using yarn (B), p18, picking up the wrap when you come to it, wrap and turn, k18.

Rows 7 and 8 Using yarn (C), [(A) for Version 2] p24, picking up the wrap when you come to it, wrap and turn, k24.

Rows 9 and 10 Using yarn (B), p30, picking up the wrap when you come to it, wrap and turn, k30.

Rows 11 and 12 Using yarn (C) [(A) for Version 2] p36, picking up the wrap when you come to it, wrap and turn, k36.

Rows 13 and 14 Using yarn (B), p42, picking up the wrap when you come to it, wrap and turn, k42.

Rows 15 and 16 Using yarn (C) [(A) for Version 2] p48, picking up the wrap when you come to it, wrap and turn, k48.

Rows 17 and 18 Using yarn (B), p54, picking up the wrap when you come to it, wrap and turn, k54.

Rows 19 and 20 Using yarn (C) [(A) for Version 2] p60, picking up the wrap when you come to it, wrap and turn, k60.

Rows 21 and 22 Using yarn (B), p67, picking up the wrap when you come to it, wrap and turn, k67.

Rows 23 and 24 Using yarn (C) [(A) for Version 2] p74, picking up the wrap when you come to it, wrap and turn, k74.

Row 25 Using yarn (B), p81, picking up the wrap when you come to it.

Row 26 Using yarn (B), k81.

Rows 27 and 28 Using yarn (C), [(A) for Version 2] p74, wrap and turn, k74.

Rows 29 and 30 Using yarn (B), p67, wrap and turn, k67.

Rows 31 and 32 Using yarn (C), [(A) for Version 2] p60, wrap and turn, k60.

Rows 33 and 34 Using yarn (B), p54, wrap and turn, k54.

Rows 35 and 36 Using yarn (C) [(A) for Version 2] p48, wrap and turn, k48.

Rows 37 and 38 Using yarn (B), p42, wrap and turn, k42.

Rows 39 and 40 Using yarn (C) [(A) for Version 2] p36, wrap and turn, k36.

Rows 41 and 42 Using yarn (B), p30, wrap and turn, k30.

Rows 43 and 44 Using yarn (C) [(A) for Version 2] p24, wrap and turn, k24.

Rows 45 and 46 Using yarn (B), p18, wrap and turn, k18.

Rows 47 and 48 Using yarn (C) [(A) for Version 2] p12, wrap and turn, k12.

Rows 49 and 50 Using yarn (B), p6, wrap and turn, k6.

Using yarn (B), purl across all 81 sts, picking up all the wraps as you come to them.

***Change back to size 10 U.S. (6 mm) and size 3 U.S. (3 mm) needles and (A) and continue for 32 rows more in Garter St. as set, dec (k2tog) 1 st at

Version 2 in Kidsilk Haze a pure silk from my stash—no finishing required.

Will-o'-the-Wisp Shawlette Schematic

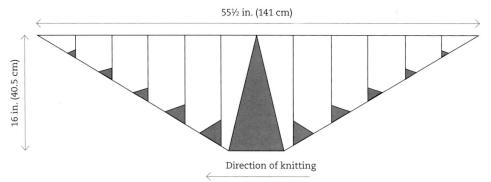

55½ in. (141 cm)

16 in. (40.5 cm)

Direction of knitting

White background—garter st in (A)
Grey triangles—Stockinette stitch short rows in (B)

beg of 2nd row, then every 4th row****—73 sts.
Change to B [(C) for Version 1], and knit across all sts.
Begin short rows:
Rows 1 and 2 P16, wrap and turn, k14, k2tog.
Rows 3 and 4 P14, wrap and turn, k12, k2tog.
Rows 5 and 6 P12, wrap and turn, k10, k2tog.
Rows 7 and 8 P10, wrap and turn, k8, k2tog.
Rows 9 and 10 P8, wrap and turn, k6, k2tog.
Rows 11 and 12 P6, wrap and turn, k4, k2tog.
Rows 13 and 14 P4, wrap and turn, k2, k2tog.
Rows 15 and 16 P2, wrap and turn, k2tog.
Row 17 Knit across all sts, picking up all the wraps as you come to them—65 sts.
Change to yarn (A) and rep from *** to ****—57 sts.
Change to yarn (B) and knit across all sts.
Begin short rows, rep rows 3–16 above.
Next row Knit across all sts, picking up all the wraps as you come to them—50 sts.
Change to (A) and rep from *** to ****—42 sts.
Change to (B) [(C) for Version 1], and knit across all sts.
Begin short rows, rep rows 5–16 above.
Next row Knit across all sts, picking up all the wraps as you come to them—36 sts.
Change to yarn (A) and rep from *** to ****—28 sts.
Change to yarn (B) [(C) for Version 1] and knit across all sts.
Begin short rows, rep rows 7–16 above.
Next row Knit across all sts, picking up

all the wraps as you come to them—23 sts.
Change to yarn (A) and rep from *** to ****—15 sts.
Change to yarn (B) [(C) for Version 1], and knit across all sts.
Begin short rows, rep rows 9–16 above.
Next row Knit across all sts, picking up all the wraps as you come to them—11 sts.
Change to yarn (A) and rep from *** to ****—3 sts.
Cast off using size 10 U.S. (6 mm) needle.

FINISHING
Weave in ends along same color rows or into side edges. Block to size on wrong side.

Optional Edging (Version 1)
Using yarn (A), crochet (p. 123) along sloping edge of shawl:
Working into spaces between ridges of Garter St., *work 1 sc, ch 3; rep from *, working ch 4 over contrast colors. Sew 3 beads onto center of each loop along edge of every contrast color.

Galaxy Beret

Swirls occur everywhere in the natural world—in vegetables, water, and galaxies. They are symbolic of the continuity and unfathomability of life. This head-hugging beret features a simple lace pattern to get you into the swirl groove. The kettle-dyed yarn gives extra zing, accentuating the horizontal dimension. It looks just as good with or without embellishment.

SKILL LEVEL
Intermediate

TIME TO KNIT
Day

FINISHED MEASUREMENTS
Small: 19 in. (48.25 cm) around brim
Medium: 21 in. (53.5 cm) around brim
Large: 23 in. (58.5 cm) around brim

Note
Pattern is written for size Small, with Medium and Large instructions in parentheses where necessary.

YARN
Rowan Colourscape Chunky
175 yd. (160 m) per 100 g hank:
1 (1, 2) hanks Northern Lights 436 or Spring 442

NOTIONS
Size 10 U.S. (6 mm) 16-in. circular needle
Size 10½ U.S. (7 mm) 16-in. circular needle
Set of four size 10 U.S. (7 mm) double-pointed needles *or size to obtain gauge*
3 buttons (optional)
Stitch markers
Tapestry needle

GAUGE
14 sts and 18 rows = 4 in. (10 cm) in Stockinette Stitch (p. 124)

TO MAKE BERET
Using size 10½ U.S. (6.5 mm) dpns, cast on 12 sts. Arrange 4 sts on each of 3 needles and join into the round.
Round 1 Knit tbl across row, placing markers before 1st and 3rd sts on each needle.
Round 2 *Sm, yo, k2, sm, yo, k2 on each needle—18 sts.
Round 3 (and all subsequent odd rows) Knit.
Round 4 *Sm, yo, k3, sm, yo, k3; rep from * around—24 sts.
Round 6 *Sm, yo, k4, sm, yo, k4; rep from * around—30 sts.
Round 8 *Sm, yo, k5, sm, yo, k5; rep from * around—36 sts.
Round 10 *Sm, yo, k6, sm, yo, k6; rep from * around—42 sts.
Round 12 *Sm, yo, k7, sm, yo, k7; rep from * around—48 sts.

continued on page 60

Round 14 *Sm, yo, k8, sm, yo, k8; rep from * around—54 sts.

Round 16 *Sm, yo, k9, sm, yo, k9; rep from * around—60 sts.

Transfer sts and markers to size 10½ U.S. (6.5 mm) circular needle, marking start of round.

Round 18 *Sm, yo, k10, sm, yo, k10; rep from * twice—66 sts.

Round 20 *Sm, yo, k11, sm, yo, k11; rep from * twice—72 sts.

Round 22 *Sm, yo, k12, sm, yo, k12; rep from * twice—78 sts.

Round 24 *Sm, yo, k13, sm, yo, k13; rep from * twice—84 sts.

Round 26 *Sm, yo, k14, sm, yo, k14; rep from * twice—90 sts.

Round 28 *Sm, yo, k15, sm, yo, k15; rep from * twice—96 sts.

Round 30 *Sm, yo, k16, sm, yo, k16; rep from * twice—102 sts.

For sizes Medium and Large, continue in this way until (34, 38) rows have been worked—(114, 126) sts.

Round 31 (35, 39) Knit to 2 sts before end of round,

Swirl Beret Schematic

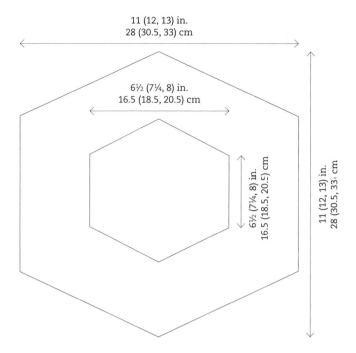

11 (12, 13) in.
28 (30.5, 33) cm

6½ (7¼, 8) in.
16.5 (18.5, 20.5) cm

6½ (7¼, 8) in.
16.5 (18.5, 20.5) cm

11 (12, 13) in.
28 (30.5, 33) cm

then start decreasing on following round:

Round 32 (36, 40) *K2tog, sm, yo, k2tog, k13 (15, 17), sm; rep from * around—96 (108, 120) sts. Cont in this way, dec 2 sts before marker at start of dec rows.

Round 34 (38, 42) *K2tog, sm, yo, k2tog, k12 (14, 16), sm; rep from * around—90 (102, 114) sts.

Round 36 (40, 44) *K2tog, sm, yo, k2tog, k11 (13, 15), sm; rep from * around—84 (96, 108) sts.

Round 38 (42, 46) *K2tog, sm, yo, k2tog, k10 (12, 14), sm; rep from * around—78 (90, 102) sts.

Round 40 (44, 48) *K2tog, sm, yo, k2tog, k9 (11, 13), sm; rep from * around—72 (84, 96) sts.

Round 42 (46, 50) *K2tog, sm, yo, k2tog, k8 (10, 12), sm; rep from * around—66 (78, 90) sts.

For Sizes Medium and Large

Round (48, 52) *K2tog, sm, yo, k2tog, k9 (11), sm; rep from * around—72 (84) sts.

For Size Large

Round 54 *K2tog, sm, yo, k2tog, k10, sm; rep from * around—78 sts.

For All Sizes

Knit next row, then change to size 10 U.S. (6 mm) circular needle and knit 9 rounds.

Next round (picot) *Yo, k2tog; rep from * around. Work 8 rounds in k1, p1 rib. Cast off loosely in rib to maintain elasticity.

FINISHING

Block lightly on WS.

Using a tapestry needle, work a running stitch around hole at center. Pull tightly to close and then fasten off securely.

Turn rib to inside of beret along picot edging and slip stitch (p. 124) in place.

If desired, attach 3 buttons in center of band below one of the 6 lace swirls.

Securely weave in ends.

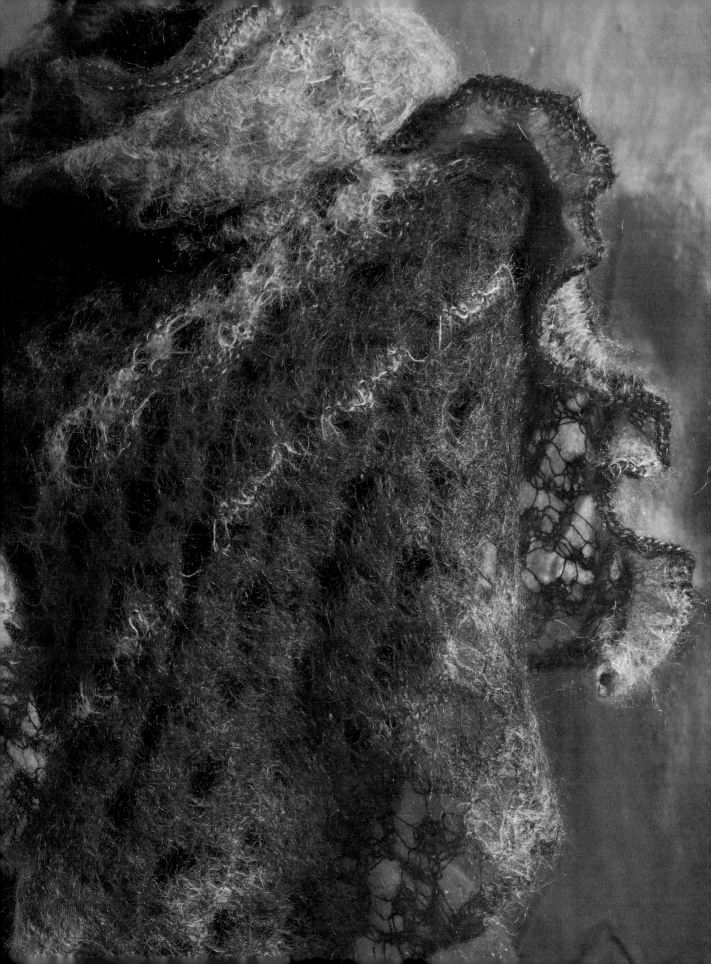

Kitten's Paw Stole

You'll find this stunning lace pattern has a relaxing rhythm to it, though I wouldn't recommend it for the beginner knitter. I've chosen two different weights of yarn. The heavier yarn is perfect for a glamorous evening wrap, while the gossamer lightweight version can also be worn as a scarf wrapped around the neck several times.

SKILL LEVEL
Advanced

TIME TO KNIT
Vacation

FINISHED MEASUREMENTS
60 in. (152 cm) long, 13 in. (33 cm) wide
(without frill)

Note
*Pattern is written for Version 1,
with Version 2 instructions in
parentheses where necessary.*

YARN
**Green Stole Version 1
(shown on p. 65)**
Rowan Kidsilk Haze Trio
153 yd. (140 m) per 50 g ball:
4 balls Fern 791

**Multicolored Stole Version 2
(shown at left)**
Rowan Kidsilk Haze Stripe
460 yd. (420 m) per 50 g ball:
2 balls Circus 205

NOTIONS
Version 1
1 pair size 8 U.S. (5 mm) needles
Size 8 U.S. (5 mm) 29-in. or 32-in. circular needle
or size to obtain gauge

Version 2
1 pair size 7 U.S. (4.5 mm) needles
Size 7 U.S. (4.5 mm) 29-in. or 32-in. circular needle
or size to obtain gauge
Stitch markers
Tapestry needle
3 yd. (3 m) 5 mm-wide silk ribbon

GAUGE
Version 1
16 sts and 23 rows = 4 in. (10 cm) in pattern using size 8 U.S. (5 mm) needles

Version 2
23 sts and 34 rows = 4 in. (10 cm) in pattern

continued on page 64

Kitten's Paw Schematic

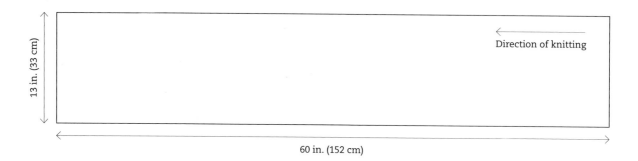

13 in. (33 cm)

Direction of knitting

60 in. (152 cm)

TO MAKE STOLE

Using straight needles, cast on 52 (76) sts, placing markers after 2nd, 14th, 26th, 38th, and 50th (62nd, 74th) sts and work in pattern:

Row 1 (RS) K2, *k2tog, yo, k2, k2tog, (yo) twice, ssk, k2, yo, ssk; rep from * to last 2 sts, k2.

Row 2 P2, *p3, p2tog-b, yo, (k1, p1) into the 2 yo's of previous row, yo, p2tog, p3; rep from * to last 2 sts, p2.

Row 3 K2, *k2, k2tog, yo, k4, yo, ssk, k2; rep from * to last 2 sts, k2.

Row 4 P2, *p3tog-b, yo, p1, yo, p4, yo, p1, yo, p3tog; rep from * to last 2 sts, p2.

Row 5 K2, *yo, ssk, k2, yo, ssk, k2tog, yo, k2, k2tog, yo; rep from * to last 2 sts, k2.

Row 6 P2, *p1, yo, p2tog, p6, p2tog-b, yo, k1; rep from * to last 2 sts, p2.

Row 7 K2, *k2, yo, ssk, k4, k2tog, yo, k2; rep from * to last 2 sts, k2.

Row 8 P2, *p2, yo, p1, yo, p3tog, p3tog-b, yo, p1, yo, p2; rep from * to last 2 sts, p2.

Rep these 8 rows until work measures 60 in. (152 cm) from cast-on edge, ending on either row 4 or 8.

Cast off using Lace Cast-Off (p. 122).

FINISHING

Press lightly under damp cloth.

Work frill along each of two side edges as foll: Divide one side edge into 10 equal 6-in. (15.25 cm) parts. With RS facing and using circular needle, pick up and k24 (33) sts in each section—240 (330) sts. Working back and forth, cont as foll:

Next row Purl.

Next row K2,*yo, k3; rep from * to last st, yo, k1—320 (440) sts.

Next row Purl.

Next row K1,*yo, k2; rep from * to last st, yo k1—480 (660) sts.

Next row Purl.

Next row Knit.

Next row Purl.

Cast off using Lace Cast-Off (p. 122).

Version 2

If cast-off edge needs to be neatened, work 1 row of sc (p. 123).

*A close-up of the stitch pattern worked in the thicker
Kidsilk Haze Trio (Version 1).*

Odalisque Turban and Hat

These retro 1920s through 1940s turbans and hats are inspired by the louche and languid odalisques in the paintings of Matisse. Basically a reconstructed two-tone scarf, the most challenging part of the pattern is actually putting it together. The design hugs the head closely, using brioche ribs for increased elasticity and working the circular part of the hat in short rows.

SKILL LEVEL
Intermediate

TIME TO KNIT
Weekend

FINISHED MEASUREMENTS
Small: 18-in. (45.75 cm) circumference
Medium: 20-in. (51 cm) circumference
Large: 22-in. (56 cm) circumference

Note
Pattern is written for size Small, with Medium and Large instructions in parentheses where necessary.

YARN
Rowan Lima
120 yd. (110 m) per 50 g ball:

Blue Turban
1 ball each Niagara 900 (A) and Amazon 879 (B)

Burgundy and Gray Turban
1 ball each La Paz 891 (A) and Argentina 893 (B)

Burgundy Hat
2 balls La Paz 891

Gray and Ecru Hat
1 ball each Bolivia 890 (A) and Argentina 893 (B)

NOTIONS
1 pair size 6 U.S. (4 mm) needles *or size to obtain gauge*
Tapestry needle

GAUGE
20 sts and 44 rows = 4 in. (10 cm) in Garter Stitch (p. 121) when blocked

TO MAKE TURBAN
Using (A), cast on 12 sts. Begin working in Brioche Rib.
Foundation row Knit.
Row 1 *K1, k1 below; rep from * to last 2 sts, k2.
Rep row 1, working 19 (21, 23) in. [48 (53.5, 58.5) cm] in Brioche Rib.
Change to yarn (B) and work 19 (21, 23) in.
[48 (53.5, 58.5) cm] more in Brioche Rib. Cast off in pattern.

TO MAKE HAT
Work as for turban, then proceed to work top of hat:
Using (A), cast on 18 (20, 22) sts.

continued on page 70

Odalisque Turban Schematic

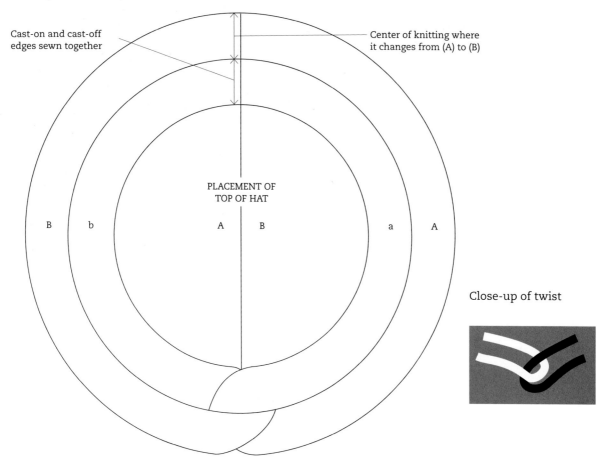

Cast-on and cast-off edges sewn together

Center of knitting where it changes from (A) to (B)

PLACEMENT OF TOP OF HAT

B   b   A   B   a   A

Close-up of twist

Large Only
Rows 1 and 2 *K20, wrap and turn, p20.
Large and Medium (Medium starts on row 3)
Rows 3 and 4 K18, wrap and turn, p18.
Large, Medium, and Small (Small starts on row 5)
Rows 5 and 6 K16, wrap and turn, p16.
Rows 7 and 8 K14, wrap and turn, p14.
Rows 9 and 10 K12, wrap and turn, p12.
Rows 11 and 12 K10, wrap and turn, p10.
Rows 13 and 14 K8, wrap and turn, p8.
Rows 15 and 16 K6, wrap and turn, p6.
Rows 17 and 18 K4, wrap and turn, p4.
Rows 19 and 20 K2, wrap and turn, p2.
Row 21 Knit across all sts, picking up loops under wrapped sts and knitting them with the st above.
Row 22 Purl across all sts**.

Rep from * to ** 4 times. Change to yarn (B) and rep 4 more times to complete the circle. Cast off. Oversew cast-on edge to cast-off edge.

FINISHING
Twist into shape as per the schematic, then stitch the two pieces together one on top of the other, stitching yarn (A) to yarn (A), yarn (B) to yarn (B), and stitching the cast-on edge to the cast-off edge at center back.

Hat
Stitch the circle to the top edge of the headband, so that yarn (A) is stitched to yarn (B) and vice versa.

Zebra Mittens

Animal prints never go out of fashion, and the zebra is one of my favorites. I'd never knit an afterthought thumb, and what a revelation it was—we knitters have so much to thank Elizabeth Zimmermann for. The fabulously soft merino and kid mohair blend yarn will keep you toasty warm and the funky stripes will make sure you stay stylish.

TIME TO KNIT
Weekend

FINISHED MEASUREMENTS
4 in. (10 cm) wide, 8½ in. (21. 5 cm) long

YARN
Rowan Cocoon
126 yd. (115 m) per 100 g ball:

Black and White Mittens
1 ball Mountain 805 (A)
1 ball Polar 801 (B)
Small amount of contrasting yarn from your stash

Lilac and Gray Mittens
1 ball Bilberry 812 (A)
1 ball Scree 803 (B)
Small amount of contrasting yarn from your stash

Teal and Gray Mittens
1 ball Mountain 805 (A)
1 ball Duck Down 833 (B)
Small amount of contrasting yarn from your stash

NOTIONS
Set of 4 size 9 U.S. (5.5 mm)
double-pointed needles
Set of 4 size 10½ U.S. (6.5 mm) double-pointed needles
or size to obtain gauge
Tapestry needle

GAUGE
18 sts. and 17 rows = 4 in. (10 cm) in Zebra Chart

TO MAKE MITTENS
Left Mitten
*Using smaller dpns and yarn (B), cast on 36 sts.
Divide sts evenly on 3 needles and join, being careful not to twist. Working in the round, work 1 row in k1, p1 rib.
Change to (A) and cont in k1, p1 rib until work measures 2 in. (5 cm).
Change to larger dpns. Refer to chart and work in Stockinette Stitch (p. 124) to end, centering chart:
Work the last 8 sts of chart, work the next 20 sts, work the first 8 sts.
When 5 rounds are completed (adjust number of rows here for larger or smaller space between top of rib and start of thumb), make a note of chart row number (this will be the row you start the thumb on) and cont for thumb:**

continued on page 70

Zebra Chart

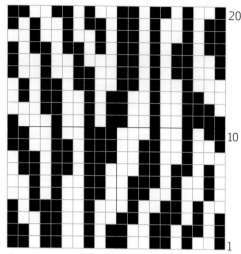

25 st repeat

Black and White Mittens

■ Mountain 805 (A)
□ Polar 801 (B)

Lilac and Grey Mittens

Bilberry 812 (A)
Scree 803 (B)

Teal and Grey Mittens

Mountain 805 (A)
Duck Down 833 (B)

Work 11 sts in pattern, then work waste yarn in different color over the next 7 sts. Slip these sts back to the LH needle, pick up the working yarn, and work across them in pattern to end of round. Work 4 in. (10 cm) in pattern (adjust length here for larger or smaller hands). Working in pattern, cont as foll:

Next round Ssk, work 14 sts, k2tog, ssk, work 14 sts, k2tog—32 sts.
Next round Ssk, work 12 sts, k2tog, ssk, work 12 sts, k2tog—28 sts.
Next round Ssk, work 10 sts, k2tog, ssk, work 10 sts, k2tog—24 sts.
Next round Ssk, work 8 sts, k2tog, ssk, work 8 sts, k2tog—20 sts.
Next round Ssk, work 6 sts, k2tog, ssk, work 6 sts, k2tog—16 sts.
Next round Ssk, work 4 sts, k2tog, ssk, work 4 sts, k2tog—12 sts.
Place first 6 sts on one needle and second 6 sts on another needle. With RSs together, work a Three-Needle Bind-Off (p. 124) with the third needle.

Work Thumb
Turn the mitten inside out. Using larger dpns, pick up the stitches for thumb along the top

and bottom of the waste yarn stitches—7 sts from the bottom and 8 sts from the top. Arrange evenly on 3 needles, then work 2¼ in. (5.75 cm) in pattern, pulling the yarn tightly at beg of each round to eliminate holes. Set chart patt as foll: Work sts 4–10 of chart, working over bottom sts and starting on the row after where waste yarn was inserted, then, working the Zebra Chart in reverse, work sts 11–4 of the same row over rem 8 sts.
When 2¼ in. (5.75 cm) have been worked, cont as foll:
K2tog around—8 sts.
Break the yarn and run it through the rem sts and pull tightly. Pull the yarn to the inside and secure.

Right Mitten
Work from * to ** as for Left Mitten, then position thumb hole:
Work waste yarn in different color over the first 7 sts of chart (sts 12–18). Slip these sts back to the LH needle, pick up the working yarn, and work across them in pattern to end of round. Cont to end as for Left Mitten.

Thumb
Pick up 15 thumb sts as before, then cont to end as for other thumb, setting chart patt as foll: Work sts 12–18 of chart (starting on row after where waste yarn was inserted) then work sts 19–12 of the same row over rem 8 sts.

FINISHING
Turn the mittens inside out and weave in any ends. Press lightly on the WS.

Stranding or weaving the yarn gives these mittens an extra layer to keep hands toasty.

CHAPTER 3

His

WHENEVER I WANT TO KNIT SOMETHING FOR ONE OF THE MEN IN my life (I have three sons), I can never find the right pattern. I'd like to save you the same trouble by sharing a selection of projects that I've long searched for.

I've tried to make the projects as versatile as possible, such as the **Hendrix Guitar Strap**, which reincarnates into a unisex belt. Then there's the **Galway Beanie and Head Wrap**—a hat with a hole, so that those with dreads or a ponytail can wear it. The **Masham Scarf** comes in a choice of rugged, undyed yarn or a floaty lightweight yarn.

Most men just love a pair of handmade socks. If this is the case with yours, the **Hugs Socks** will do the job. Made in a chunky Aran weight, they'll get you up to speed with Fair Isle. If Fair Isle's not your bag, just omit it, and you'll have a stylish plain pair with stripes at top, toe, and heel.

Finally, there's the **Tutti-Frutti Smartphone Sleeve**, a basic cover that can be customized with an icon of your choice.

Featured techniques include Fair Isle, intarsia, cables, knots, knitting with odd needles, and fringes for finishing.

Hugs Socks

I've never known a man who can resist a pair of knitted socks, and if they're Fair Isle socks, then that's a bonus. This cozy pair is robust enough to wear either with or without shoes; the decorative striping in the heel does a good job of reinforcing it. For a less pronounced striped effect, swap the colors in the chart around to give a consistent background throughout, as in the second version.

SKILL LEVEL
Intermediate

TIME TO KNIT
Weekend

FINISHED MEASUREMENTS
Small: To fit small-sized man's foot
Large: To fit medium-sized man's foot

Note
Pattern is written for size Small, with Large instructions in parentheses where necessary.

YARN
Rowan Felted Tweed Aran
95 yd. (87 m) per 50 g ball:

Blue Socks (Colorway 1)
2 balls of Storm Blue 730 (A)
1 ball of Pebble 720 (B)

Gray Socks (Colorway 2)
2 balls of Dusty 728 (A)
1 ball of Soot 729 (B)

NOTIONS
Set of 4 size 6 U.S. (4 mm) double-pointed needles
Set of 4 size 7 U.S. (4.5 mm) double-pointed needles
Set of 4 size 8 U.S. (5 mm) double-pointed needles
or size to obtain gauge
Stitch markers
Tapestry needle

GAUGE
16 sts and 23 rows = 4 in. (10 cm) in Stockinette Stitch (p. 124)

Note
For information on knitting Fair Isle, see p. 121.

TO MAKE LEG
Using size 7 U.S. (4.5 mm) needles and yarn (A), cast on 40 sts using the Continental Cast-On (p. 120) to give an elastic edge. Change to size 6 U.S. (4 mm) needles and divide the sts evenly onto 3 needles. Place marker at beg of round, then join in the round, being careful not to twist sts.
Knit 1 round tbl in yarn (A), then work 4 rows in bicolored rib, taking care not to strand the yarn too tightly on the back of work:
Round 1 *K2 using yarn (A), p2 using yarn (B), rep from * around.

continued on page 76

Hugs Chart

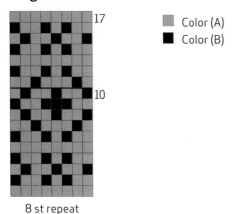

17

10

■ Color (A)
■ Color (B)

8 st repeat

Change to size 8 U.S. (5 mm) needles, then work
17 rounds of Hugs Chart as foll:
Round 1 Work the 8 sts of Hugs Chart 5 times.

Note
For a different look with no contrasting stripe,
swap the colors in the chart as in Gray Socks.

When chart is completed, cont in Stockinette St.
using yarn (A), working decs on first round as foll:
For size Small: Ssk, k4, (ssk, k5) 4 times, ssk,
k4—34 sts.
For size Large: (Ssk, k18) twice—38 sts.
When work measures 7½ in. (19 cm) from
cast-on edge, turn the work inside out and work
in opposite direction to finish sock, wrapping yarn
when you change direction to avoid a hole.

Divide for Heel

Place the first 8 (9) sts and the last 9 (10) sts
of the round onto one needle for the heel.
Place the remaining 17 (19) sts onto another
needle for the instep. Work heel sts:
Row 1 With RS facing, join both yarns. *K1 (A),
k1 (B). Rep from * ending k1 (A). Turn.
Row 2 *P1 (A), p1 (B). Rep from * ending
with p1 (A). Turn.
Rep these 2 rows 5 more times.

Note
Slip the first st on every row except the first.

Turn Heel

Foundation row (RS) Work in pattern for
11 (13) sts, skpo (sl 1, k1, psso), turn.
Row 1 (WS) Sl 1, work in pattern for
5 (7) sts, p2tog, turn.
Row 2 (RS) Sl 1, work in pattern for
5 (7) sts, skpo, turn.
Rep rows 1 and 2 until all the sts have been
worked. Turn work so that RS is facing
for next row.

Shape Gussets

Place 17 (19) instep sts on one needle and
the rem 7 (9) sts for heel on another needle.
With RS facing and using yarn (A), knit the heel sts,
then:
Needle 1: Using a new needle and yarn (A),
pick up and knit 8 sts along the selvage of the heel,
using the loops made by slipping the first sts.
Needle 2: Using a new needle and yarn (A), knit
across the instep sts.
Needle 3: Using a new needle and yarn (A),
pick up and knit 8 sts along the selvage of the heel,
using the loops made by slipping the first sts.
With the same needle, knit 4 (5) sts from the
needle with the heel sts.
Transfer the rem 3 (4) sts onto Needle 1.

The Fair Isle socks are knit in the round with the right side always facing so you can see the pattern as it develops.

Round 1

Needle 1: Using yarn (A), knit to last 3 sts, k2tog, k1.

Needle 2: Using yarn (A), knit.

Needle 3: Using yarn (A), k1, skpo, knit to end.

Round 2 Knit.

Rep these 2 rounds until there are 34 (38) sts. Continue to knit in Stockinette St. until work measures 6½ (7) in. [16.5 (18) cm] from start of gusset, or until foot length measures 2 in. less than desired finished length.

Shape Toe

Distribute sts on dpns:

Needle 1: 8 (9) sts starting at the center of the heel.

Needle 2: 17 (19) sts over the top of the foot.

Needle 3: 9 (10) rem sts.

Round 1

Needle 1: Using yarn (B), knit to 3 sts from the end, k2tog, k1.

Needle 2: K1, ssk, knit to last 3 sts from the end of needle, k2tog, k1.

Needle 3: K1, ssk, knit to end of round.

Round 2 Using yarn (A), knit.

Rep these last 2 rounds until there are 4 (5) sts on needle 1, 9 (11) sts on needle 2, and 5 (6) sts on needle 3. Continuing in stripes pattern, rep round 1 (dec round only) until there is 1 st on needle 1, 3 sts on needle 2, and 2 sts on needle 3.

Break yarn, leaving a 10-in. (25.5 cm) tail. Thread a tapestry needle. Draw it through the remaining 6 sts. Tighten on inside to finish the toe. Securely weave ends into like colors.

Masham Scarf

This is one of the easiest of knits—it's in Garter Stitch with no finishing at all. Natural undyed yarn will appeal to the man in your life who appreciates the rugged outdoors and has a no-frills attitude to gifts. Or choose a lightweight yarn to transform the same pattern into a delicate, floating scarf that's perfect for a woman to wear on a breezy summer's evening. I've used different-sized needles to create openness and texture, and different colors, too. Make one for him and one for you.

SKILL LEVEL
Beginner

TIME TO KNIT
Day

FINISHED MEASUREMENTS
45 in. (114 cm) long, 5 in. (12.75 cm) wide

YARN
His Scarf (Version 1)
Rowan British Sheep Breeds Fine Bouclé
109 yd. (100 m) per 50 g ball:
1 ball Masham Stripe 319 (A)
1 ball Light Brown Masham 317 (B)

Her Scarf (Version 2)
Rowan Kidsilk Haze
229 yd. (210 m) per 25 g ball:
1 ball Candy Girl 606 (A)
1 ball Blushes 583 (B)

NOTIONS
His Scarf
One pair size 9 U.S. (5.5 mm) needles
or size to obtain gauge

Her Scarf
1 each of size 3 U.S. (3.25 mm) and size 15 U.S. (10 mm) needles, used as a pair
or size to obtain gauge

GAUGE
14 sts and 24 rows = 4 in. (10 cm)
in Garter Stitch (p. 121)

Note
Slip the first stitch and knit into the back of the last stitch on every row to make selvage.

TO MAKE SCARF
Version 1
Using yarn (A), cast on 18 sts.
Rows 1–18 Using yarn (A), work in Garter St.
Rows 19–36 Change to yarn (B) and cont in Garter St.
Rep rows 1–36 seven times.
Work 18 more rows in yarn (A). Cast off—270 rows.

continued on page 80

Masham Scarf Schematic

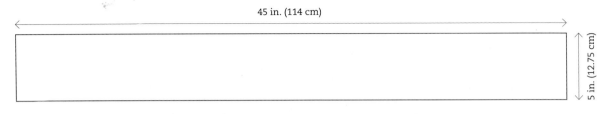

45 in. (114 cm)

5 in. (12.75 cm)

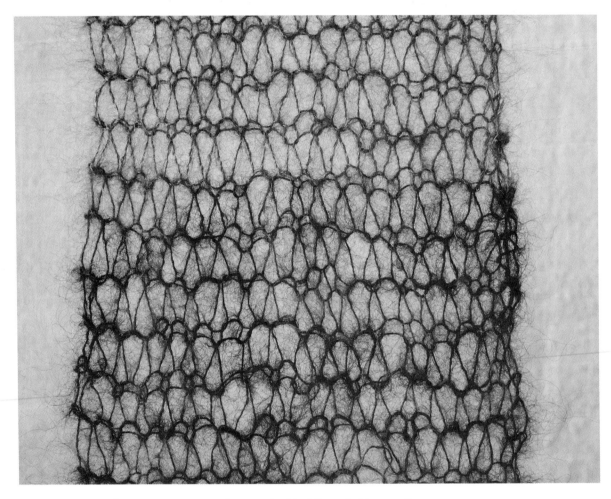

Different-sized needles create openness and texture in this delicate-looking scarf.

Version 2

Using yarn (A) and size 15 U.S. (10 mm) needles, cast on 18 sts. Cont as for Version 1, working next row with size 3 needle, then size 15 needle for following row. Cont alternating rows with the two different-sized needles to end. Cast off using size 15 U.S. (10 mm) needles.

FINISHING

Securely weave ends into like colors. Press lightly to size on WS.

Galway Beanie and Head Wrap

There's always an occasion to wear a cozy Aran hat—fishing, gardening, painting the porch, bringing in the logs, or pounding the pavement to keep fit. These are all good activities to encourage—leaving you more time to curl up and knit! The alternative head wrap version is perfect for dreadlocks or a ponytail—why not knit one for yourself as well?

SKILL LEVEL
Advanced

TIME TO KNIT
Weekend

FINISHED MEASUREMENTS
Extra-Small: 17-in. (43 cm) circumference
Small: 19-in. (48 cm) circumference
Medium: 20½-in. (52 cm) circumference
Large: 22-in. (56 cm) circumference

Note
Pattern is written for size Extra-Small, with Small, Medium, and Large instructions in parentheses where necessary.

YARN
Rowan Felted Tweed Aran
95 yd. (87 m) per 50 g ball:
2 (2, 3, 3) balls Cherry 732 (Beanie)
2 (2, 3, 3) balls Storm Blue 730 (Head Wrap)

NOTIONS
1 pair size 7 U.S. (4.5 mm) needles
or size to obtain gauge
Cable needle
Tapestry needle

GAUGE
25 sts and 25 rows = 4 in. (10 cm) in cable pattern

TO MAKE BEANIE (SHOWN IN RED)
Using smaller needles, cast on 105 (118, 131, 144) sts and begin cable pattern.
Row 1 P1, k1, p1, k8, *p1, k1, p1, k1, p1, k8; rep from * 7 (8, 9, 10) times, p1, k1, p1.
Rows 2, 4, 6, and 8 K1, p1, k1, *p8, k1, p1, k1, p1, k1; rep from * 7 (8, 9, 10) times, p8, k1, p1, k1.
Row 3 P1, k1, p1, place 4 sts on cn and hold at front of work, k4, k4 from cn, *p1, k1, p1, k1, p1, place 4 sts on cn and hold at front of work, k4, k4 from cn, rep from * 7 (8, 9, 10) times, p1, k1, p1.
Rows 5 and 7 P1, k1, p1, k8, *p1, k1, p1, k1, p1, k8; rep from * 7 (8, 9, 10) times, p1, k1, p1.
Rep these 8 rows until work measures 6 (6½, 7, 7½) in. [15.25 (16.5, 17.75, 19) cm] from cast-on edge, ending on WS row.

continued on page 84

Shape Crown

At the same time, keep cables correct every 8th row.

Row 1 K1, p2tog, k8, *p1, s2kpo, p1, k8; rep from * 7 (8, 9, 10) times, p1, k2tog—89 (100, 111, 122) sts.

Row 2 P1, k1, *p8, k1, p1, k1; rep from * 7 (8, 9, 10) times, p8, k1, p1.

Row 3 K1, p1, k8, *p1, k1, p1, k8; rep from * 7 (8, 9, 10) times, p1, k1.

Row 4 P1, k1, *p8, k1, p1, k1; rep from * 7 (8, 9, 10) times, p8, k1, p1.

Row 5 K1, p1, ssk, k4, k2tog, *p1, k1, p1, ssk, k4, k2tog; rep from * 7 (8, 9, 10) times, p1, k1—73 (82, 91, 100) sts.

When you subsequently come to the cable row, it will be over 6 sts after this row:
Place 3 sts on cn and hold at front of work, k3, k3 from cn.

But if the cable falls on the same row as the dec, row 5 will read:
K1, p1, place 4 sts on cn and hold at front, ssk, k2; k2, k2tog from cn, [p1, k1, p1, place 4 sts on cn and hold at front, ssk, k2; k2, k2tog from cn] 7 (8, 9, 10) times, p1, k1—73 (82, 91, 100) sts.
Work cable every 6 rows from now on.

Row 6 P1, k1, *p6, k1, p1, k1; rep from * 7 (8, 9, 10) times, p6, k1, p1.

Row 7 K1, p1, ssk, k2, k2tog, *p1, k1, p1, ssk, k2, k2tog; rep from * 7 (8, 9, 10) times, p1, k1—57 (64, 71, 78) sts.
If the cable falls on this row: K1, p1, place 3 sts on cn and hold at front, ssk, k1; k1, k2tog from cn, *p1, k1, p1, place 3 sts on cn and hold at front, ssk, k1; k1, k2tog from cn; rep from * 7 (8, 9, 10) times, p1, k1.

Row 8 P1, k1, *p4, k1, p1, k1; rep from * 7 (8, 9, 10) times, p4, k1, p1.

Row 9 K1, p1, *ssk, k2tog, p1, k1, p1; rep from * 7 (8, 9, 10) times, ssk, k2tog, p1, k1—41 (46, 51, 56) sts.
If the cable falls on this row: Place 2 sts on cn and hold at front of work, ssk, k2tog from cn.

Row 10 P1, k1, *p2, k1, p1, k1; rep from * 7 (8, 9, 10) times, ssk, k2tog, k1, p1.

Row 11 K1, p1, *ssk, p1, k1, p1; rep from * 7 (8, 9, 10) times, ssk, p1, k1—33 (37, 41, 45) sts.

The ribbed cable creates a stretchy but snug fabric to hug the head and keep you cozy.

Row 12 *P1, k1; rep from * to last st, p1.

Row 13 K1, *k3tog, k1; rep from * 8 (9, 10, 11) times—17 (19, 21, 23) sts.

Row 14 P2tog to last st, p1.
Break off yarn and thread through rem 9 (10, 11, 12) sts. Pull tightly and secure on inside.

TO MAKE HEAD WRAP (SHOWN IN BLUE ON P. 83)
Work as for Beanie, casting off loosely in pattern on row 10.

FINISHING
Oversew back seam on inside.

Tutti-Frutti
Smartphone Sleeve

No prizes for guessing what inspired this design. If you do need a clue, it's in the fruit. Not wishing to invite copyright issues, I decided that an apple is not the only fruit. Feel free to take the pear as a jumping-off point for other icons and customize as you like. For those knitters who can't face intarsia, skip the fruit and instead stripe the sleeve with leftovers from your stash.

SKILL LEVEL
Beginner/Intermediate

TIME TO KNIT
Day

FINISHED MEASUREMENTS
4½ in. (11.5 cm) long, 2½ in. (6.5 cm) wide

Note
If your phone is slightly larger or smaller, you can add or subtract a few rows before the motif.

YARN
Rowan Cotton Glace
125 yd. (115 m) per 50 g ball:

Black Sleeve
1 ball Black 727 (A)
1 ball Bleached 726 (B)

Orange Sleeve
1 ball Blood Orange 445 (A)
1 ball Dawn Grey 831 (B)

Gray Sleeve
1 ball Umber 838 (A)
1 ball Oyster 730 (B)

Blue Sleeve
1 ball Twilight 829 (A)
1 ball Sky 749 (B)

NOTIONS
1 pair size 3 U.S. (3.25 mm) needles
or size to obtain gauge
Tapestry needle

GAUGE
24 sts and 32 rows = 4 in. (10 cm) in Stockinette Stitch (p. 124)

Note
For more information on knitting intarsia, see p. 122.

continued on page 86

Tutti-Frutti Chart

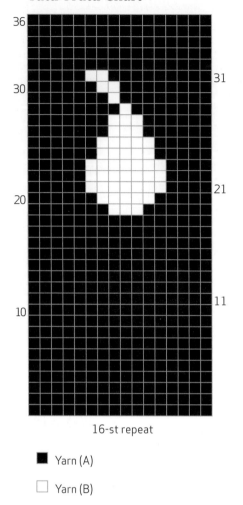

36
31
30
21
20
11
10

16-st repeat

■ Yarn (A)

□ Yarn (B)

Tutti-Frutti Smartphone Sleeve Schematic

2½ in. (6.5 cm)

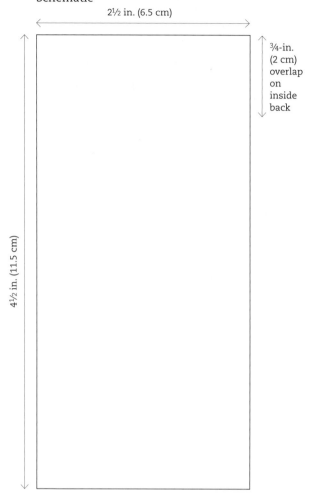

¾-in. (2 cm) overlap on inside back

4½ in. (11.5 cm)

TO MAKE SLEEVE

Back

Using yarn (A), cast on 16 sts. Refer to Tutti-Frutti Chart and work the 36 rows in Stockinette St.
Rows 37 and 38 Using yarn (A), purl to form foldline.
Work 6 rows more in Stockinette St.
Cast off knitwise.

Front

Using yarn (A), cast on 16 sts. Work 36 rows in Stockinette St., then cast off knitwise.

FINISHING

Turn down the 6 rows above the foldline to the inside on back and stitch in place along both side edges. With RS together, oversew front to back around three sides, leaving top open.
Weave in ends securely on the WS. Press lightly on the WS.

Customize the sleeve with any icon you'd like, or skip the intarsia completely.

Hendrix Guitar Strap
and Linen Belt

While a guitar strap and belt are suitable gifts for any gender, I decided to place them in this section. The linen yarn gives the guitar strap a minimum stretch, and both versions are adjustable to fit.

SKILL LEVEL
Intermediate

TIME TO KNIT
Day

FINISHED MEASUREMENTS
Guitar Strap
2¾ in. (7 cm) wide, 50 in. (127 cm) long

Linen Belt
Extra-Extra Small: 38 in. (96.5 cm) long, 2¾ in. (7 cm) wide
Extra-Small: 40 in. (101.5 cm) long, 2¾ in. (7 cm) wide
Small: 42 in. (106.5 cm) long, 2¾ in. (7 cm) wide
Medium: 44 in. (111.5 cm) long, 2¾ in. (7 cm) wide
Large: 46 in. (116.5 cm) long, 2¾ in. (7 cm) wide
Extra-Large: 48 in. (121.5 cm) long, 2¾ in. (7 cm) wide

Note
Pattern is written for size Extra-Extra Small, with Extra-Small, Small, Medium, Large, and Extra-Large instructions in parentheses where necessary.

YARN
Rowan Creative Linen
219 yd. (200 m) per 100 g hank:

Guitar Strap
1 hank Salmon 627 (A)
1 hank Carbonised 639 (B)

Linen Belt
1 hank Natural 621 (A)
1 hank Carbonised 639 (B)

NOTIONS
1 pair size 7 U.S. (4.5 mm) needles
or size to obtain gauge
Size G-6 U.S. (4 mm) crochet hook
Tapestry needle
2 yd. (2 m) Petersham ribbon, 2 in. wide
(for the guitar strap)
1 button (for the belt)

GAUGE
24 sts and 28 rows = 4 in. (10 cm) in cable pattern
22 sts and 28 rows = 4 in. (10 cm) in Stockinette Stitch (p. 124)

SPECIAL ABBREVIATIONS
Knot Stitch
Using yarn (B), p1, k1, p1, k1, p1 into st, making 5 sts from 1, then pass the 2nd, 3rd, 4th, and 5th sts over the first st.

continued on page 90

Hendrix Guitar Strap Schematic

50 in. (127 cm)

2¾ in. (7 cm) ↕ | I I I I I |

Linen Belt Schematic

38 (40, 42, 44, 46, 48) in.
96.5 (101.5, 106.5, 111.5, 116.5, 121.5) cm

2¾ in. (7 cm) ↕ | I I I I I |

TO MAKE GUITAR STRAP
Cast on 18 sts in yarn (A), then 14 sts in
yarn (B)—32 sts

Note
*When changing colors in middle of a row, twist the
yarns around each other to avoid holes.*

Row 1 (and all WS rows) Using yarn (B),
sl 1, p13. Change to yarn (A) and k1, p16, k1tbl.
Row 2 Using yarn (A), sl 1, sl next 4 sts onto cn and
hold at back of work, k4, k4 from cn, sl next 4 sts
onto cn and hold at front of work, k4, k4
from cn, k1. Change to yarn (B) and k13, k1tbl.
Row 4 Using yarn (A), sl 1, k17. Change to yarn (B).
K13, k1tbl.
Row 6 Using yarn (A), sl 1, k8. Change to yarn (B).
Work Knot St. on next st. Change to yarn (A) and
k8. Change to yarn (B) and k13, k1tbl.
Row 8 Rep row 4.
Rep these 8 rows to end, working buttonhole
rows as foll:
**Rows 10, 18, 26, 34, 42, and 50 (buttonhole
rows)** Using yarn (A), sl 1, sl next 4 sts onto cn and
hold at back of work, k4, k4 from cn, sl next
4 sts onto cn and hold at front of work, k4, k4 from
cn, k1. Change to yarn (B) and k5, cast off 4,
k4, k1tbl.
Cast on over the cast-off sts when you come to
them on next row.
Cont until work measures 49 in. (124.5 cm) from
cast-on edge when slightly stretched, ending on
row 1 (lengthen or shorten to fit here if necessary),

then work a further buttonhole row as before.
Work another 9 rows, ending on row 3. Cast off.

FINISHING
Press to shape lightly on WS. Fold strap lengthwise
along center knit st and oversew in place on inside
along side edge. Insert a length of ribbon approx.
43 in. (109 cm) to strengthen strap from top of 6th
buttonhole to bottom of last buttonhole, sewing
down back of strap to hold the ribbon in place
along the length of the strap.
Oversew strap top and bottom.
Stitch around buttonholes to hold together
and neaten.

Fringe
Add fringe to 6-buttonhole end of strap:
Cut eight 12-in. (30 cm) lengths of yarn (A) and ten
12-in. (30 cm) lengths of yarn (B). Place 2 lengths of
the same color together. Put crochet hook through
beginning of cast-on edge from back to front, pull
center of 2 pieces of yarn through, then put the
ends of yarn through the loop created. Pull tightly.
Alternate yarn (A) and (B) fringes across cast-on
edge. Trim to neaten.

Note
No fringe on opposite end.

If you'd prefer to, you can omit the knots and let the cable stand center stage.

Linen yarn gives great stitch definition.

TO MAKE BELT

Work as for guitar strap until work measures 38 (40, 42, 44, 46, 48) in. [96.5 (101.5, 106.5, 111.5, 116.5, 121.5) cm] from cast-on edge when slightly stretched, ending on row 3 and omitting final buttonhole 1 in. (2.5 cm) from the end. Cast off.

FINISHING

Attach button at cast-off end. Omit the ribbon and the fringe.

CHAPTER 4

Home

FOR MOST OF US, THE VERY SOUND OF THE WORD HOME MAKES us feel warm and safe. It's a place where we can recharge our batteries. The projects I've chosen here resonate with the spirit of the home.

What better way to greet our friends and visitors than with the **Welcome Toran**? This colorful door hanging would make any guest feel at home. There's also **Flavor**, an easy-to-knit place mat and napkin ring set to give your dinner party guests the VIP treatment.

I love teapots and the whole ritual surrounding tea—a packet of loose-leaf Earl Grey is one of the greatest little gifts. So this chapter wouldn't be complete without the **Wensleydale Tea Cozy**. If you're fond of taking tea in the garden like me, the **Checkers Cushion and Seat Cover** will make sure you're comfy.

No home is complete without a pet. We have two young Maine Coon cats, Django and Arlo, but having thick, well-insulated coats, they present few knit design opportunities. I love dogs, too, so it was a real thrill to try my hand at designing the **McDougal Dog Jacket**.

Checkers Cushion and Seat Cover

Get up to speed on your shadow knitting with these cushion covers. Watch and wonder as they change from striped to checkerboard depending on the angle from which they're viewed. A tied-on seat cover is sure to pretty up any kitchen chair, and the cushions, with their quirky frog buttons, can be relied upon to create a talking point on any sofa.

SKILL LEVEL
Intermediate

TIME TO KNIT
Weekend

FINISHED MEASUREMENTS
Small: 12½ in. (32 cm) wide, 12½ in. (32 cm) long
Large: 15½ in. (39.5 cm) wide, 15½ in. (39.5 cm) long

Note
Pattern is written for size Small, with Large instructions in parentheses where necessary.

YARN
Rowan Creative Linen
219 yd. (200 m) per 100 g hank:

Small Cushion
1 (2) hank Salmon 627
1 (2) hank Natural 621

Large Cushion
1 (2) hank Carbonised 639
1 (2) hank Cloud 620

Seat Cover
1 (2) hank Leaf 632
1 (2) hank Apple 629

NOTIONS
1 pair size 5 U.S. (3.75 mm) needles
1 pair size 7 U.S. (4.5 mm) needles
Size 7 U.S. (4.5 mm) 29-in. or 32-in. circular needle (for Seat Cover only) *or size to obtain gauge*
Stitch markers
Tapestry needle
3 (4) buttons (for Cushion only)
Pillow insert (for Cushion only)
Optional piece of foam rubber (for Seat Cover only)

GAUGE
20 sts and 32 rows = 4 in. (10 cm) in Checkers Chart

Note
Slip the first stitch and knit into the back of the last stitch on every row to make selvage.

TO MAKE CUSHION
Back
Using size 7 U.S. (4.5 mm) needles and yarn (A), cast on 62 (77) sts.
Work the Checkers Chart, placing markers every 15 sts (excluding the first and last sts) and work as follows:

continued on page 96

Checkers Chart

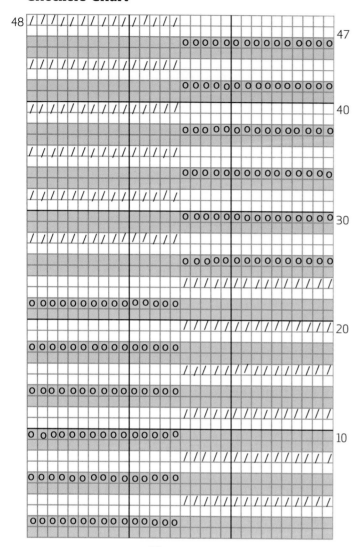

30-st repeat

■ Using (A), knit

ο Using (A), purl

□ Using (B), knit

/ Using (B), purl

For Small size
Row 1 Sl 1, work the 30 sts of chart twice, k1tbl.
Row 2 Sl 1, work the 30 sts of chart twice, k1tbl.
Work the 48 rows twice, then work rows 1 and
2—98 rows.*
Next row Using size 5 U.S. (3.75 mm) needles and
yarn (A), purl across row.

For Large size
Row 1 Sl 1, work the 30 sts of chart twice, work the
first 15 sts, k1tbl.
Row 2 Sl 1, work the last 15 sts of chart, work the
30 sts of chart twice, k1tbl.
Work the 48 rows twice, then work 26 rows more—
122 rows.*
Next row Using size 5 U.S. (3.75 mm) needles and
yarn (A), purl across row.

Both sizes
To make the button band, change back to size U.S.
7 (4.5 mm) needles. Using yarn (A) and starting

Checkers Cushion Schematic

12 (15) in./30 (38) cm

12 (15) in./30 (38) cm

with a purl row, work in Stockinette St. for 9 rows more. Cast off.

Front

Work 1 and 2 rows as for Cushion Back, and then proceed as follows:

Work the 48 rows 1 (2) times, then work 44 (20) rows of Checkers Chart—92 (116) rows.

Continuing in Checkers Chart, work buttonhole as follows:

Next row (buttonhole row) Work first 13 sts, cast off next 3 sts 3 (4) times, work 14 (13) sts.

Next row Work in pattern, casting on 3 sts over those cast off on previous row.

Work 4 more rows in pattern.

Next row (RS) Using size 5 U.S. (3.75 mm) needles and yarn (A), purl 1 row.

Change to size 7 U.S. (4.5 mm) needles. Starting with a purl row, work in Stockinette St. and (A) to end.

Work 4 rows, then work buttonhole rows as before, starting on WS row.

Work 3 more rows. Cast off.

TO MAKE SEAT COVER

Back

Using size 7 U.S. (4.5 mm) needles and yarn (A), cast on 62 (77) sts and work 12¼ in. (31 cm) [15¼ in. (38.75 cm)] in Garter St. (p. 121). Cast off loosely.

Front

Work as for back of Seat Cover to *.
Cast off in yarn (A).

FINISHING

Backstitch (p. 118) on edge of work to firm seams.
Lay work flat and block on WS.

To Finish Seat Cushion

With RS together, join three sides, leaving buttonhole side open. Fold the button and buttonhole bands to inside along purl row and slip stitch (p. 124) in place. Turn Seat Cushion right side out and attach buttons on button band opposite buttonholes. Neaten buttonholes. Insert pillow insert into Seat Cushion.

continued on page 99

Shadow knitting uses only stripes of knit and purl stiches to trick the eye into believing the colors are changing.

Unique buttons allow you to personalize the gift.

To Finish Seat Cover

With RS together, join four sides, leaving a 4-in. (10 cm) opening at end to pull cover through to outside. Sew 4-in. (10 cm) opening neatly on outside. If preferred, cover can be stuffed with a thin layer of foam rubber.

Using size 7 U.S. (4.5 mm) circular needle and yarn (A), cast on 62 (77) sts using a Cable Cast-On (p. 119) to make seat cover tie.

With RS facing and starting at top left-hand corner of cover, pick up and knit 62 (77) sts along three sides of cover, working neatly into seam. Cast on a final 62 (77) sts as before—310 (385) sts. Cast off all of these sts loosely.

Using size 7 U.S. (4.5 mm) circular needle and yarn (A), cast on 62 (77) sts using a Cable Cast-On. Pick up and knit 62 (77) sts along top seam of cover. Cast on a final 62 (77) sts using Cable Cast-On—186 (231) sts. Cast off sts loosely. Securely weave in all ends.

Flavor Place Mat and Napkin Ring

Showcase your knitting skills next time you have friends to dinner with fine dining on these easy Stockinette place mats and Garter Stitch napkin rings. I've used a linen/cotton mix, which gives glorious stitch definition. The napkin rings make a great stand-alone gift too. To make them extra special, choose buttons with a theme relevant to the recipient, *et voilà*, a unique last-minute gift, with time to spare.

SKILL LEVEL
Beginner

TIME TO KNIT
Day

FINISHED MEASUREMENTS
Place Mat: 18¾ in. (45 cm) wide, 13¾ in. (35 cm) long
Napkin Ring: 2½ in. (6.5 cm) wide, 8 in. (20.5 cm) long

YARN
Rowan Creative Linen
219 yd. (200 m) per 100 g hank:
1 hank each Salmon 627, Leaf 632, Natural 621, or Carbonised 639

Note
One hank will make four place mats and four napkin rings.

NOTIONS
1 pair size 5 U.S. (3.75 mm) needles
1 pair size 7 U.S. (4.5 mm) needles *or size to obtain gauge*
1 button
Tapestry needle

GAUGE
20 sts and 24 rows = 4 in. (10 cm) in Stockinette Stitch (p. 124)
20 sts and 32 rows = 4 in. (10 cm) in Garter Stitch (p. 121)

Note
Knit the first stitch and knit into the back of the last stitch on every row to form selvage.

TO MAKE PLACE MAT
Using smaller needles, cast on 68 sts and work in Garter St. for 6 rows. Change to larger needles and continue in Stockinette St.:
RS rows Knit.
WS rows K4, p60, k4.
Continue until work measures 18 in. (45.75 cm) from cast-on edge, ending on WS row.
Change to smaller needles and work 6 rows in Garter St.
Cast off loosely knitwise, making sure the work does not pull in along cast-off edge.

FINISHING
Weave in ends securely on the WS.
Press lightly on the WS.

continued on page 102

Flavor Place Mat Schematic

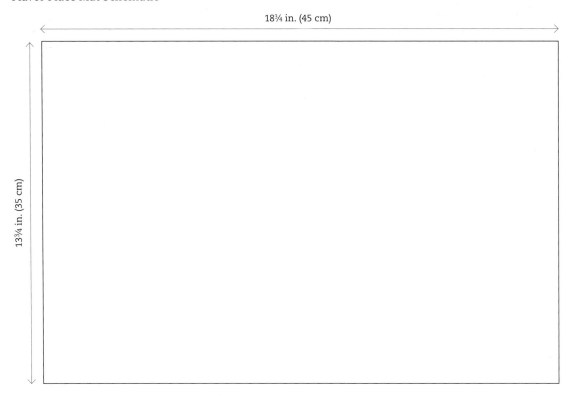

18¾ in. (45 cm)

13¾ in. (35 cm)

Flavor Napkin Ring Schematic

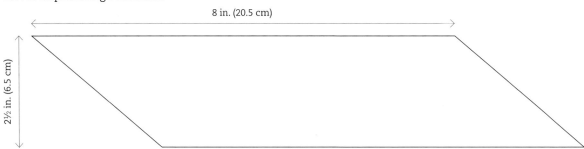

8 in. (20.5 cm)

2½ in. (6.5 cm)

TO MAKE NAPKIN RING
Using larger needles, cast on 1 st.

Note
Check that shaping at beg and end is neat,
as there is no finishing on this piece.

Row 1 (RS) Knit into front and back of this 2 sts.
Row 2 (WS) Knit into front and back of first st,
k1—3 sts.
Row 3 K2, knit into front and back of last st—4 sts.

Row 4 Knit into front and back of first st, k3—5 sts.
Row 5 K4, knit into front and back of last st—6 sts.
Row 6 Knit into front and back of first st, k5—7 sts.
Row 7 K6, knit into front and back of last st—8 sts.
Row 8 Knit into front and back of first st, k7—9 sts.
Row 9 K8, knit into front and back of last st—
10 sts.
Row 10 Knit into front and back of first st, k9—
11 sts.
Row 11 K10, knit into front and back of last st—
12 sts.

The place mat in Leaf and napkin ring in Natural.

Row 12 Knit into front and back of first st, k11—13 sts.

Continue in Garter St. until piece measures 6¼ in. (16 cm) from cast-on edge, ending on WS row.

Continue as follows:

Row 1 K5, cast off 3 to form buttonhole, k5.

Row 2 Knit, casting on 3 sts over the space left by cast-off sts.

Rows 3 and 4 Knit.

Row 5 K2tog, k11—12 sts.

Row 6 K10, k2tog—11 sts.

Row 7 K2tog, k9—10 sts.

Row 8 K8, k2tog—9 sts.

Row 9 K2tog, k7—8 sts.

Row 10 K6, k2tog—7 sts.

Row 11 K2tog, k5—6 sts.

Row 12 K4, k2tog—5 sts.

Row 13 K2tog, k3—4 sts.

Row 14 K2, k2tog—3 sts.

Row 15 K2tog, k1—2 sts.

Row 16 K2tog—1 st.

Cast off remaining st.

FINISHING

Weave in ends securely on the WS.

Press lightly on the WS.

Attach button in appropriate place to fit napkin.

Wensleydale Tea Cozy

On our most recent Lakes and York knitters' tour, I noticed the Wensleydale Longwool Sheepshop had their own tea cozies decorated with fleece from their flock. When I asked if I could get some, they helpfully sent me hand-dyed colors to match yarn I wanted to use. This pattern is an opportunity to polish your tuck skills in simple Stockinette, with medium and large sizes offering the possibility of easy conversion into hats—just omit the hole for the spout.

SKILL LEVEL
Intermediate

TIME TO KNIT
Weekend

FINISHED MEASUREMENTS
Extra-Small: 13-in. (33 cm) circumference at base
Small: 15-in. (38 cm) circumference at base
Medium: 18-in. (45.75 cm) circumference at base
Large: 19-in. (48.25 cm) circumference at base
Extra-Large: 20-in. (51 cm) circumference at base

Note
Height is variable due to the rolled base. Pattern is written for size Extra-Small, with Small, Medium, Large, and Extra-Large instructions in parentheses where necessary.

YARN
Rowan Creative Focus Worsted
220 yd. (200 m) per 100 g ball:

New Fern with Multicolored Tucks Colorway (shown p. 107)
Background: (A)
Tuck Sequence: (B), (C), (D), (E), (F)
1 (1, 1, 2, 2) balls New Fern 01265 (A)
1 ball each True Purple 01800 (B), Magenta 01890 (C), Syrah 02025 (D), Copper 02190 (E), and Teal 03360 (F)

Magenta Colorway (shown p. 104, top left)
Background: (C)
Tuck Sequence: (A), (B)
1 (1, 1, 2, 2) balls Magenta (C)
1 ball each New Fern (A) and True Purple (B)

True Purple Colorway (shown p. 104, bottom left)
Background: (B)
Tuck Sequence: (C), (D), (E)
1 (1, 1, 2, 2) balls True Purple (B)
1 ball each Magenta (C), Syrah (D), Copper (E)

Teal Colorway (shown p. 104, bottom right)
Background: (F)
Tucks: (A)
1 (1, 1, 2, 2) balls Teal (F)
1 ball New Fern (A)

continued on page 106

NOTIONS

1 size 3 U.S. (3.25 mm) needle for picking up tuck row
1 pair size 7 U.S. (4.5 mm) needles *or size to obtain gauge*
Size G-6 U.S. (4 mm) crochet hook
Stitch holders
Tapestry needle
1 packet of Wensleydale Longwool Sheepshop or other dyed fleece for decoration

GAUGE

20 sts and 24 rows = 4 in. (10 cm) in Stockinette Stitch (p. 124)

TO MAKE TEA COZY

Using background color and larger needles, cast on 65 (75, 90, 95, 100) sts and work 8 rows in Stockinette St.
Change to relevant contrast color (see p. 105) and work 9 rows more in Stockinette St.

Tuck

Using smaller needle, pick up the sts on the WS through the loops of the first row of contrast color.
Tuck row (WS) Place RH needle in first st as if to purl, then put needle through first st of picked-up sts as if to purl, and purl together. Rep this across row, forming a tuck on RS.
Change to background color and cont in Stockinette St., working 32 (37, 45, 47, 50) sts to end. Place the rem sts on a holder.
Work 3 more rows. Change to next relevant contrast color and work 9 rows, then work another tuck as before.
*Change to background color and work 4 rows, then change to next relevant contrast color. Work 9 rows, then work tuck as before**.

Sizes Medium, Large, and Extra-Large

Rep from * to ** twice, using next 2 relevant contrast colors respectively. Place these sts on holder.
Rejoin yarn to other 32 (37, 45, 47, 50) sts and work similarly to match.

Next row (RS) Rejoin yarn and, using yarn background color, knit across sts on first holder, then across sts on second holder—65 (75, 90, 95, 100) sts.
Next row Purl.
Next row *K2tog, k3; rep from * across row—52 (60, 72, 76, 80) sts.
Next row Purl.
Change to next relevant contrast color and work 9 rows. Then work tuck as before. Change to background color and work 2 rows, then cont as foll:
Next row *K2tog, k2; rep from * across row—39 (45, 54, 57, 60) sts.
Next row Purl.
Cont in next relevant contrast color and work 9 rows. Then work tuck as before. Change to background color and work 2 rows, then cont as foll:
Next row *K2tog, k1; rep from * across row—26 (30, 36, 38, 40) sts.
Next row Purl.
Change to next relevant contrast color and work 9 rows. Then work tuck as before. Change to background color and work 2 rows then cont as foll:
Next row K2tog across row—13 (15, 18, 19, 20) sts.
Next row Purl.
Next row K2tog across row—7 (8, 9, 10, 10) sts.
Break yarn, leaving a long tail. Run tail through rem sts and secure on inside.

FINISHING

Oversew side seam on inside, leaving hole for spout. Close and neaten the ends of each tuck around holes in same color. Join any tucks on the seam.

Note

All teapots are different, so try the cozy on your teapot to fit to spout and handle.

Have fun experimenting with tucks—for a different look try just three tucks at the base of the cozy, finishing it off in stockinette.

Make Tassels

Make 3 (4, 5, 6, 6) tassels, using each color:

Cast on 20 sts over 2 needles held together to create a loose cast-on. Slide one needle out and continue as follows:

Knit into front and back, then front again of every st across row—60 sts.

Cast off purlwise.

Use your fingers to twirl the tassels into shape.

Work 1 row of sc (p. 123) in background color around handle and spout holes.

Sew fleece and tassels securely to top of tea cozy.

McDougal Dog Jacket

Pets are important members of the family, so here's the perfect gift for a furry friend. This jacket was test knitted by Jenny, who's the proud guardian of a rescue dog named Dougal. When Jenny completed the jacket, she was delighted to find it fit Dougal like a glove. The pattern is a full-on intarsia knit, but because the yarn is thick, you don't have to juggle too many balls on the back.

SKILL LEVEL
Advanced

TIME TO KNIT
Vacation

FINISHED MEASUREMENTS
Extra-Extra-Small: 16 in. (41 cm) chest, 13 in. (33 cm) long from collar to tail
Extra-Small: 18 in. (46 cm) chest, 14 in. (36 cm) long from collar to tail
Small: 20 in. (51 cm) chest, 16 in. (41 cm) long from collar to tail
Medium: 22 in. (56 cm) chest, 18 in. (46 cm) long from collar to tail
Large: 24 in. (61 cm) chest, 20 in. (51 cm) long from collar to tail
Extra-Large: 26 in. (67 cm) chest, 23 in. (59 cm) long from collar to tail
Extra-Extra-Large: 28 in. (72 cm) chest, 24 in. (61 cm) long from collar to tail

Note
Pattern is written for size Extra-Extra-Small, with Extra-Small, Small, Medium, Large, Extra-Large, and Extra-Extra-Large instructions in parentheses where necessary.

YARN
Rowan Drift
87 yd. (80 m) per 100 g ball:

Colorway 1 (not shown)
1 (1, 1, 1, 1, 1, 1) ball Shore 908 (A)
1 (1, 1, 1, 1, 1, 1) ball Solo 910 (B)
1 (1, 1, 1, 2, 2, 2) balls Fire 906 (C)
1 (1, 1, 1, 2, 2, 2) balls Windy 909 (D)
1 (1, 1, 1, 1, 1, 1) ball Plantation 905 (E)
1 (1, 1, 1, 1, 1, 1) ball Nomad 907 (F)

Colorway 2 (shown at right)
1 (1, 1, 1, 1, 1, 1) ball Shore 908 (A)
1 (1, 1, 1, 1, 1, 1) ball Fire 906 (B)
1 (1, 1, 1, 2, 2, 2) balls Nomad 907 (C)
1 (1, 1, 1, 2, 2, 2) balls Plantation 905 (D)
1 (1, 1, 1, 1, 1, 1) ball Windy 909 (E)
1 (1, 1, 1, 1, 1, 1) ball Solo 910 (F)

NOTIONS
1 pair size 11 U.S. (8 mm) needles
1 pair size 15 U.S. (10 mm) needles *or size needed to obtain gauge*
Size L-11 U.S. (8 mm) crochet hook
Stitch holders
Tapestry needle
Hook-and-loop tape

GAUGE
10 sts and 14 rows = 4 in. (10 cm)
in Stockinette Stitch (p. 124)

Note
For more information on Intarsia knitting, see p. 122.

continued on page 110

McDougal Colorway 1 Chart

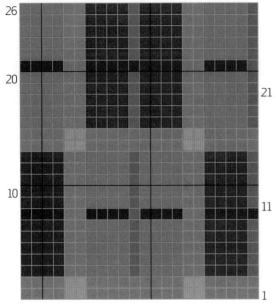

22-st repeat

■ Shore 908 (A)
■ Solo 910 (B)
■ Fire 906 (C)
■ Windy 909 (D)
■ Plantation 905 (E)
■ Nomad 907 (F)

McDougal Colorway 2 Chart

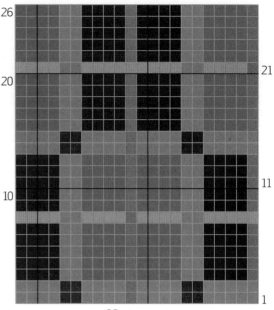

22-st repeat

■ Shore 908 (A)
■ Fire 906 (B)
■ Nomad 907 (C)
■ Plantation 905 (D)
■ Windy 909 (E)
■ Solo 910 (F)

TO MAKE JACKET

Using smaller needles and yarn (A), cast on
30 (34, 40, 44, 50, 54, 60) sts and work 2 rows
in Garter St. (p. 121).

Change to larger needles. Refer to McDougal
Colorway 1 Chart or McDougal Colorway 2 Chart
and rep the 26 rows to end, centering the pattern:

RS rows Work the last 4 (6, 9, 0, 3, 5, 8) sts, work
the 22 sts of chart 1 (1, 1, 2, 2, 2, 2) times,
work the first 4 (6, 9, 0, 3, 5, 8) sts of chart—
30 (34, 40, 44, 50, 54, 60) sts.

WS rows Work as above, working from left to right
across chart until work measures 6 (7, 8, 9, 10, 11,
12) in. [15.25 (17.75, 20.25, 23, 25.5, 28, 30.5) cm]
from cast-on edge, ending on WS row.

Strap

Using Cable Cast-On (p. 119), cast on 6 sts at beg
of next row, work in pattern to end, then using
Backward Loop Cast-On (p. 119), cast on 8 sts—
44 (48, 54, 58, 64, 68, 74) sts.

Work 3 in. (7.5 cm), ending on a WS row.

Starting on the WS row, center chart as foll:

WS rows Work the last 12 (14, 17, 8, 11, 13, 16) sts,
work the 22 sts of chart 1 (1, 1, 2, 2, 2, 2) time, work
the first 10 (12, 15, 6, 9, 11, 14) sts of chart—44 (48,
54, 58, 64, 68, 74) sts.

RS rows Work the last 10 (12, 15, 6, 9, 11, 14) sts
of chart, work the 22 sts of chart 1 (1, 1, 2, 2, 2, 2)
times, work the first 12 (14, 17, 8, 11, 13, 16) sts
of chart.

McDougal Schematic

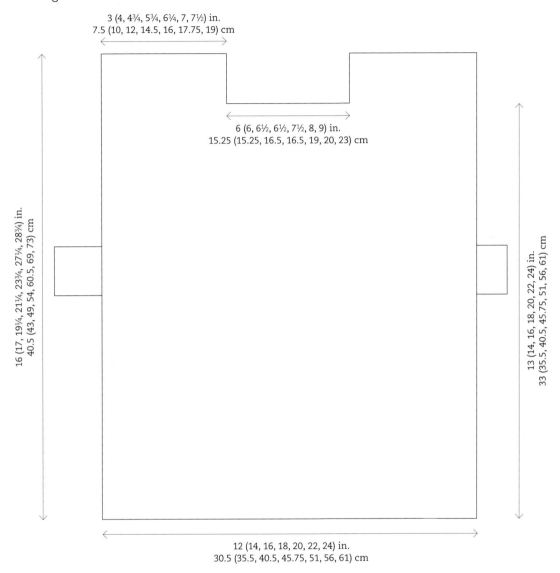

3 (4, 4¾, 5¾, 6¼, 7, 7½) in.
7.5 (10, 12, 14.5, 16, 17.75, 19) cm

6 (6, 6½, 6½, 7½, 8, 9) in.
15.25 (15.25, 16.5, 16.5, 19, 20, 23) cm

16 (17, 19¼, 21¼, 23¾, 27¼, 28¾) in.
40.5 (43, 49, 54, 60.5, 69, 73) cm

13 (14, 16, 18, 20, 22, 24) in.
33 (35.5, 40.5, 45.75, 51, 56, 61) cm

12 (14, 16, 18, 20, 22, 24) in.
30.5 (35.5, 40.5, 45.75, 51, 56, 61) cm

When 3 in. (7.5 cm) have been worked, cont in pattern:

Next row Cast off 6 sts, work in pattern as set to end.

Next row Cast off 8 sts, work in pattern as set to end—30 (34, 40, 44, 50, 54, 60) sts.

Cont in pattern as set until work measures 13 (14, 16, 18, 20, 23, 24) in. [33 (35.5, 40.5, 45.75, 51, 56, 61) cm].

Shape Neck

Keeping pattern as set, work 8 (8, 12, 14, 16, 17, 19) sts, cast off 14 (14, 16, 16, 18, 20, 22) sts for neck, place rem 8 (8, 12, 14, 16, 17, 19) sts on holder.

WS rows Work last 8 (8, 12, 14, 16, 17, 19) sts.

RS rows Work first 8 (8, 12, 14, 16, 17, 19) sts.

Rep these rows until work measures 16 (17, 19¼, 21¼, 23¾, 27¼, 28¾) in. [40.5 (43, 49, 54, 60.5, 69, 73) cm].

continued on page 112

For beginner knitters stripes are a good alternative—these heathery hues will zing just as well if you play around with the width of the stripes.

Cast off in pattern.
Rejoin yarn to sts on the stitch holder and continue in pattern to match other side:
RS rows Work last 8 (8, 12, 14, 16, 17, 19) sts.
WS rows Work first 8 (8, 12, 14, 16, 17, 19) sts.

FINISHING
Neckband
Using smaller needles and yarn (B), with RS facing and starting at right front edge, pick up and k10 (10, 11, 11, 13, 15, 17) sts along side edge of neck, pick up and k14 (14, 16, 16, 18, 20, 22) sts at center neck, and pick up and k10 (10, 11, 11, 13, 15, 17) sts along other neck edge—34 (34, 38, 38, 44, 50, 56) sts. Work 1 in. (2.5 cm) in k1, p1 rib and then cast off in rib to maintain elasticity.

Oversew the 2 cast-off edges and side edges of rib together neatly on inside. Using yarn (B), work one row of sc (p. 123) around the entire jacket, including strap. Sew a strip of hook-and-loop tape outside the shorter strap and sew the other piece inside the longer strap so that the longer strap fastens on top of the shorter strap in a position to fit your dog comfortably.
If required to secure, use ch sts to work a crocheted loop at center of cast-on edge to fit under tail.

Welcome Toran
Door Hanging

The toran is a Hindu or Buddhist door hanging that both welcomes guests to your home and celebrates events like weddings, births, and traditional festivals. Flamboyantly adorned with flowers, leaves, and mirrors, the toran symbolically blesses everyone who walks beneath with an abundance of love, prosperity, health, and happiness.

SKILL LEVEL
Intermediate

TIME TO KNIT
Vacation

FINISHED MEASUREMENTS
Small: 20 in. (51 cm) wide, 13 in. (33 cm) long
Medium: 28 in. (71 cm) wide, 13 in. (33 cm) long
Large: 36 in. (91.5 cm) wide, 13 in. (33 cm) long

Note
Pattern is written for size Small, with Medium and Large instructions in parentheses where necessary.

YARN
Rowan Cotton Glacé
125 yd. (115 m) per 50 g ball:
1 ball each Cobalt 850 (A), Ultramarine 851 (B), Winsor 849 (C), Bubbles 724 (H), and Toffee 843 (J)

Rowan Wool Cotton
123 yd. (113 m) per 50 g ball:
1 ball each Elf 946 (D), Brolly 980 (E), and Rich 911 (G)
1 (2, 2) balls Café 985 (F)

Note
I used yarn from my stash, so some colors above are the closest matches I could find in current yarns.

NOTIONS
1 pair size 3 U.S. (3.25 mm) needles
Size 3 U.S. (3.25 mm) 29-in. or 32-in. circular needle
or size to obtain gauge
Size G-6 U.S. (4 mm) crochet hook
Stitch holders and markers
Tapestry needle

GAUGE
24 sts and 32 rows = 4 in. (10 cm) in Stockinette Stitch (p. 124)

Note
For more information on Intarsia knitting, see p. 122.

continued on page 114

Welcome Toran Chart

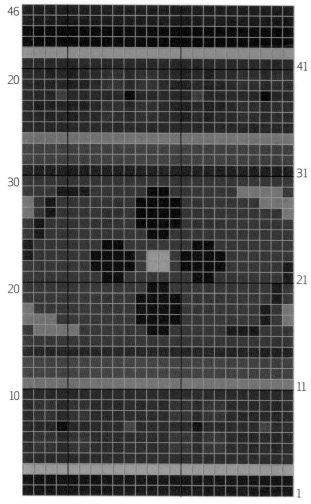

46
41
20
30
31
20
21
10
11
1

24-st repeat

- ■ Cobalt 850 (A)
- ■ Ultramarine 851 (B)
- ■ Winsor 849 (C)
- ■ Elf 946 (D)
- ■ Brolly 980 (E)
- ■ Café 985 (F)
- ■ Rich 911 (G)
- ■ Bubbles 724 (H)
- ■ Toffee 843 (J)

Cont on these sts until work measures 7 in. (17.75 cm), ending on WS row. Place sts on stitch holder.

Top

With RS facing, use extra-long size 3 U.S. (3.25 mm) needle and yarn (J) to pick up and knit 23 sts from the flags in the foll sequence:

Small: (J), (G), (E), (D), (B), casting on 1 st between each flag and 1 st at the end of the row—120 sts.

Medium: (J), (G), (F), (E), (D), (B), (A), casting on 1 st between each flag and 1 st at the end—168 sts.

Large: (J), (H), (G), (F), (E), (D), (C), (B), (A), casting on 1 st between each flag and 1 st at the end—216 sts.

Next row Purl.

Refer to Welcome Toran Chart and work the 46 rows, rep the 24 sts of the chart 5 (7, 9) times across row.

Cast off.

TO MAKE TORAN

Flags

Small: Make 5 flags in colors (B), (D), (E), (G), and (J).

Medium: Make 7 flags in colors (A), (B), (D), (E), (F), (G), and (J).

Large: Make 9 flags in colors: (A), (B), (C), (D), (E), (F), (G), (H), and (J).

Using size 3 U.S. (3.25 mm) needles, make a slip knot and place on needle. Work in front, back, and front again of this st—3 sts.

Working in Stockinette St., increase 1 st at both ends of every other row until there are 23 sts.

FINISHING

Weave in any ends securely on the WS.

Press lightly on the WS.

Starting at top RH corner, with RS facing and using 2 strands of yarn (F), work 1 row of sc (p. 123) along top of piece, down side edge of top, around each of the flags, and finishing at top of side edge where you started. Using 2 strands of yarn (F), work 6 ch sts in each top corner to make loops for hanging. Embellish with mirrors, jewels, or beads according to preference.

Welcome Toran Schematic

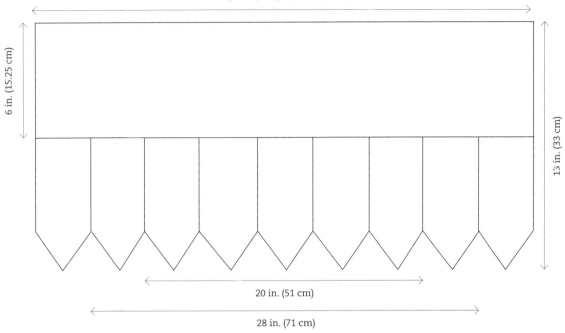

20 (28, 36) in. [51 (71, 91.5) cm]

6 in. (15.25 cm)

13 in. (33 cm)

20 in. (51 cm)

28 in. (71 cm)

Flags are only attached to the top border, not each other.

If intarsia's not your thing, remember you can substitute with either Swiss darning, embroidery, or jewels and beads.

APPENDIX I

Techniques and Stitches

Attaching Beads

For attaching beads, I prefer the slip stitch method, as it ensures that the bead stays on the right side of the work.

On a RS row, work to the position of the beaded stitch. Bring the yarn forward to the front of the work and push a bead down the yarn so that it lies against the needle at the front of the work. Slip the next stitch purlwise, leaving the bead in front of the slipped stitch. Take the yarn to the back and continue to work as normal.

On a WS row, work to the position of the bead, take the yarn to the back of the work, and place the bead so that it lies on the RS of work against the needle. Slip the next stitch purlwise, leaving the bead behind the slipped stitch. Take the yarn to the front and continue to purl as set.

NOTE: The Big Eye needle is wonderful for threading the beads. As its name suggests, it's one gigantic flexible eye. If you can't find one, then thread a fine needle with about 8 in. (20 cm) of cotton thread and knot the two ends together. Thread the yarn through the loop of cotton thread, and off you go.

Backstitch

Use a small, neat backstitch on the inside of the selvage stitch to create a stable, strong seam when sewing piece together.

Place right sides together and insert needle from back to front between first and second rows. Pull yarn through. Insert needle from front to back between the first row and cast-on edge, then from back to front between the second and third rows. Pull yarn through, then *insert needle from front to back at end of last backstitch (one row back), then from back to front two rows forward. Pull yarn through. Rep from * to end.

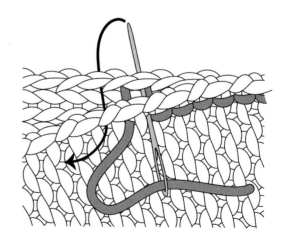

Backward Loop Cast-On

This simple cast-on is useful for casting on stitches in the middle of a row. It's sometimes used for making a stitch between stitches.

Make a backward loop and place it on the needle. Repeat as many times as required.

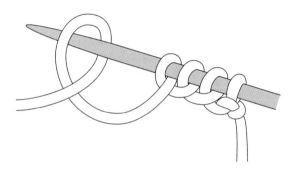

Blocking and Pressing

Never underestimate the power of blocking and pressing! Small mistakes often become invisible when a piece is well presented. Some projects need pressing more than others, so I've included specific instructions to press in some projects.

Before blocking, neaten the selvages by sewing or weaving in all the ends along the sides or along color joins where appropriate. Then, using pins, block each piece of knitting to shape— this also gives you an opportunity to check the measurements. Gently press each piece on the WS, omitting ribbing, using a warm iron and a damp pressing cloth. Take special care with the edges.

Cable Cast-On

This is a useful cast-on when stitches need to be added within your work.

Make a slip knot on the LH needle. Working into this knot's loop, knit 1 st and place it on the LH needle.

Insert the RH needle between the last 2 sts. From this position, knit 1 st and place it on the LH needle. Rep this step to cast on each additional st.

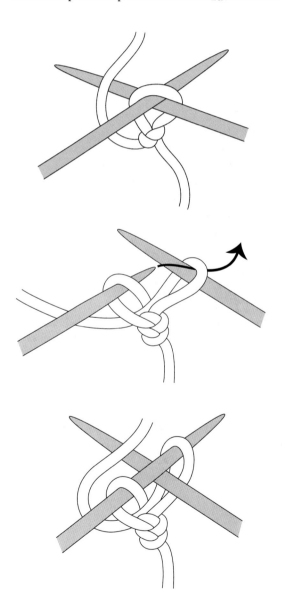

Cables

Cabling is simply a way of crossing one set of stitches over another set and looks best when worked against a contrasting background stitch, like working a Stockinette Stitch cable on a reverse Stockinette Stitch background. Basic cables are worked by placing the first set of stitches on a cable needle and holding them at the back or front of your knitting, depending on whether you want the crossing to slope toward the right or left. Holding the stitches at the front will result in a left-sloping cable, and holding them at the back will yield a right-sloping cable. For example, here's a 4-stitch cable that slopes to the left:

On a RS row, work to the position of the cable and sl the next 2 sts onto the cable needle, holding it at the front of the work.

Working behind the cable needle, knit the next 2 sts from the LH needle.

Now knit the 2 sts from the cable needle to create a crossover to the left.

Chart Reading

When knitting back and forth, charts are read from right to left on RS rows and from left to right on WS rows. Charts can begin with a RS or WS row; this will be indicated by where row 1 is situated on the chart. For instance, if row 1 is on the left, then the chart starts with a WS row; if it is on the right, it starts with a RS row. In circular knitting, all rows are RS rows and every row is read from right to left.

Every square (or rectangle) in a chart represents 1 stitch horizontally and 1 row vertically. The symbols inside each square represent either stitches (knit, purl, cable, and so on) or colors (in intarsia or two-color stranded knitting). When working with several colors, it's good to tape a small piece of each color alongside its symbol so you have a constant reminder of which yarn to use.

To keep track of your place in the chart, use a premade line finder or make one yourself by taking a strip of card or plastic the width of the chart and cut a long slit into it, approximately the size of a row. This window can then be moved up the chart as you knit, masking the rows you've knitted and highlighting the one you're working on. If the size of a chart is too small for comfortable reading as printed in the book, enlarge it using a photocopier before you start the project.

Color Slip Stitch Knitting

Slip stitch designs are an easy way to begin knitting with color. This technique uses two or more colors, but only one strand is ever used at a time. The pattern is made by the extra-long stitches made by slipping certain stitches. Give it a try on the Deco Backpack (p. 50).

There are only two things to remember: On RS rows, slip the stitches with yarn at back of work. On WS rows, slip the stitches with yarn at front of work.

Yarn is always on the WS for slipped stitches. Some patterns call for the slipped stitches to be carried on the RS, producing a bar, but these are much less common.

Continental (Long-Tail) Cast-On

Make a slip knot for the initial st, at a distance from the end of the yarn about 1 in. (2.5 cm) for each st to be cast on. Arrange both ends of the yarn in the left hand as shown on the facing page.

Bring the needle under the front strand of the thumb loop, up over the front strand of the index finger loop, catching the yarn on the needle. Bring the same needle under the front of the thumb

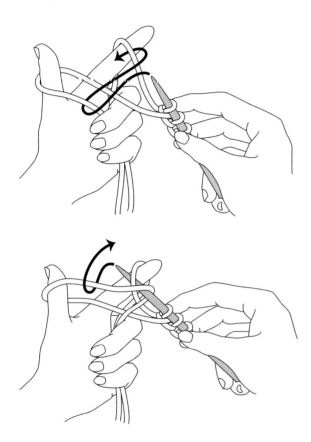

which the working yarn is held in the right hand, and the Continental method (picking the yarn), in which it is held in the left hand. This produces an even, pleasing effect and is wonderfully rhythmic when working in the round, where all rows are knit rows.

However, when knitting back and forth, I've found that a lot of knitters have a problem with the tension on the purl side. A speedy and even alternative is to use either circular or double-pointed needles and work across the row, knitting every Color A stitch and slipping (purlwise) every Color B stitch. Do not turn the work at the end of the row, but instead slide the stitches back to the right-hand point of the needle, drop Color A, pick up Color B, and work every stitch that should be Color B, slipping every stitch that was previously worked in Color A. Then turn the work and proceed in the same way on the purl side. When working in the round, work one round with Color A and then one round with Color B to complete each single row. If you always smoothly stretch out the slipped stitches on the right-hand needle before stranding the yarn, this method makes it easy to control the tension of the strands and avoids any puckering of the fabric. Do not strand the yarn over more than 3 stitches.

loop. Slip the thumb out of the loop, and use it to adjust the tension on the new st—1 st cast on.

Rep this process until all sts are cast on.

Fair Isle (Two-Color Stranded Knitting)

Many knitters remain in awe of this technique, but once you have mastered Stockinette Stitch, you are ready for Fair Isle. It's just a matter of organizing your yarn and making sure you don't pull the yarn too tightly to maintain elasticity in the knitted fabric. The nonworking yarn is carried loosely on the wrong side, either woven in or stranded.

In my workshops, I usually teach the two-handed method, but this involves working simultaneously with the British method (throwing the yarn), in

French Knot

Bring needle from back to front of work, wrap yarn around needle 10 times, use thumb to hold yarn in place while pulling needle through wraps, then pass needle through to back of work in place where it emerged and fasten off.

Garter Stitch

Knit all rows or purl all rows.

Garter Stitch in the Round

Round 1 Knit.
Round 2 Purl.
Rep these 2 rounds.

I-Cord

Cast on 3 sts using a double-pointed needle, *slide these sts to the other end of the needle, then knit them using the yarn brought around from the other end. Rep from * to end.

Intarsia

A way of getting as many colors as you're able to handle into one row, this technique was once called picture knitting. It can create wonderful designs and it's not difficult, but it can be fiddly and therefore off-putting to new knitters. Try it out on the Tutti-Frutti Smartphone Sleeve (p. 85) or take the plunge with the McDougal Dog Jacket (p. 108)— if you find you enjoy the process, there's a huge pot of gold at the end of this knitting rainbow!

If the design has a background color, use separate balls of yarn for each of the contrast colors, stranding or weaving the main color behind. This cuts down on the number of ends to weave in later and gives the contrast colors a slightly raised effect, which helps define the pattern.

For intarsia with random shapes, use a separate length of yarn for each color every time it occurs, twisting the two colors around each other at each color change to avoid creating holes in the knitting. To eliminate tangles, wrap each length around a bobbin and let it dangle on the back of the work or use short lengths of yarn (no longer than 24 in. [61 cm]) and straighten at the end of each row.

Lace Cast-Off

K1, *pass this st back to LH needle and k2tog; rep from * to end.

Lace Cast-On

Make a slip knot. *Knit into the slip knot, but do not slip the st off the LH needle. Place the new st on the LH needle; rep from * until there are the required number of sts.

Moss Stitch

Row 1 *K1, p1; rep from * to end.
On all subsequent rows, purl the knit sts and knit the purl sts.

Picking Up Stitches around a Neckline

To get a professional finish on a neckline, it's important to pick up and knit evenly, with no bunching or stretching of stitches. Sometimes, due to the design of a pattern, stitches are left live at the center back and/or center front, but unless the pattern calls for this, it's generally best to cast off. The reason for this is that all the stress of the garment when worn will be falling away from the center back neck; therefore, necklines tend to stretch and become bigger than intended. One way of countering this is to do a firm cast-off at the center back and front neck edges.

To pick up a stitch from a cast-off edge, hold the knitting with the right side toward you, insert the needle under an edge stitch, wrap the yarn around, and pull a loop through to make a stitch.

Pick up the number of stitches indicated in the pattern, and remember that the next row will be a WS row.

Picot Point Cast-Off

Cast off 1 (2) sts, *slip rem st on RH needle onto LH needle, cast on 1 (2) sts, cast off 3 (4) sts; rep from * to end and fasten off rem st.

Reverse Stockinette Stitch

Purl on RS rows, knit on WS rows.

Selvage Edges

Always work a selvage on every row when possible. This helps prevent curl and makes finishing easier (especially when sewing pieces together), as the resulting notches can be matched. There are many different selvage stitches, but old habits die hard, and I usually use the beaded selvage my grandmother taught me:

Sl the first st knitwise and knit into the back of the last st on every row.

Another good stitch to use is the chain selvage, which is great for backstitch seams and also helps when picking up stitches or working crochet edges:

RS rows Sl the first st knitwise and knit the last st.

WS rows Sl the first st purlwise and purl the last st.

Take time to experiment and find the selvage stitch that works for you.

Single Crochet (UK Double Crochet)

I often use crochet to finish off a project. In this book I use the U.S. term *single crochet*; UK knitters should remember that terminology for basic crochet stitches like *single crochet* and *double crochet* in the U.S. translates into *double crochet* and *treble crochet*, respectively, in the UK.

Make a slip knot to begin.

Insert the hook into the next st.

Yo and pull a loop through the next st indicated in the pattern—2 loops are on the hook.

Yo and pull a loop through both loops on the hook, 1 single crochet completed.

Rep steps 1–3 as instructed in the pattern (see illustrations below).

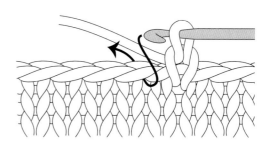

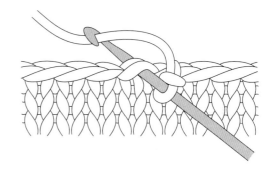

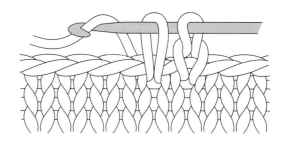

Slip Stitch

I usually join the ribs and neckband with a slip stitch so that they lie flat. This method is suitable for any yarn weight except bulky.

Working with the two wrong sides facing you, catch one or two strands from the edge of the top piece, then one or two strands from the edge of the other piece. Don't pull the yarn too tightly.

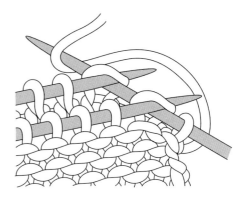

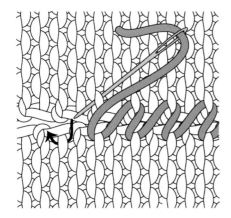

Stockinette Stitch

Knit on RS rows and purl on WS rows.

Stockinette Stitch in the Round

Knit every round.

Three-Needle Bind-Off

This is a neat way of joining seams on the inside or decoratively on the outside, especially if the shoulder shaping uses short rows.

Place the work RS together, with the back sts on 1 needle and front sts on another. *Work 2 tog (1 from front needle and 1 from back needle). Rep from * once.

Cast off the first st over the 2nd st. Continue to work 2 sts tog (1 front st and 1 back st) and cast off across.

Wrapping a Stitch

On a knit row:

With yarn in back, sl the next st as if to purl. Bring the yarn to the front of the work and sl the st back to the LH needle. Turn the work.

Work the row as instructed in the pattern, and when you come to the wrap on the following knit row, make it less visible by knitting it together with the st it wraps.

For more information on any of the techniques used, video tutorials are available to purchase at www.jeanmoss.com.

Yarn Information

PLEASE DON'T WORRY IF YOU CAN'T SOURCE THE EXACT yarn. These projects are the perfect excuse for an afternoon spent exploring your stash. All of my patterns give the yardage of the suggested yarn. If you can roughly match this and have checked that gauge and handle are compatible by swatching, there's no reason why you shouldn't use an alternative.

Numbers in brackets correspond with yarn weight symbols in the Standard Yarn Weight System chart, p. 126.

Rowan Baby Merino Silk DK
147 yd. (135 m) per 50 g ball:
66% merino superwash wool, 34% tussah silk
[CYCA 3]

Rowan British Sheep Breeds Fine Bouclé
109 yd. (100 m) per 50 g ball:
91% British wool, 9% nylon [CYCA 4]

Rowan Big Wool
87 yd. (80 m) per 100 g ball:
100% merino wool [CYCA 6]

Rowan Cashsoft DK
126 yd. (115 m) per 50 g ball:
57% extra fine merino wool, 33% acrylic microfiber, 10% cashmere [CYCA 3]

Rowan Cocoon
126 yd. (115 m) per 100 g ball:
80% merino wool, 20% kid mohair [CYCA 5]

Rowan Colourscape Chunky
175 yd. (160 m) per 100 g skein:
100% lambswool [CYCA 5]

Rowan Cotton Glacé
126 yd. (115 m) per 50 g ball:
100% cotton [CYCA 3]

Rowan Creative Focus Worsted
220 yd. (200 m) per 100 g ball:
75% wool, 25% alpaca [CYCA 4]

Rowan Creative Linen
219 yd. (200 m) per 100 g hank:
50% linen, 50% cotton [CYCA 4]

Rowan Drift
87 yd. (80 m) per 100 g ball:
100% merino wool [CYCA 6]

Rowan Felted Tweed Aran
95 yd. (87 m) per 50 g ball:
50% merino wool, 25% alpaca, 25% viscose
[CYCA 4]

Rowan Fine Lace
437 yd. (400 m) per 50 g ball:
80% baby suri alpaca, 20% fine merino wool
[CYCA 1]

Rowan Handknit Cotton
93 yd. (85 m) per 50 g ball:
100% cotton [CYCA 4]

Rowan Kidsilk Haze
229 yd. (210 m) per 25 g ball:
70% super kid mohair 30% silk
[CYCA 3]

Rowan Kidsilk Haze Stripe
460 yd. (420 m) per 50 g ball:
70% super kid mohair, 30% silk
[CYCA 3]

Rowan Kidsilk Haze Trio
153 yd. (140 m) per 50 g ball:
70% super kid mohair, 30% silk
[CYCA 4]

Rowan Lima
109 yd. (100 m) per 50 g ball:
84% baby alpaca, 8% merino wool, 8% nylon
[CYCA 4]

Rowan Panama
148 yd. (135 m) per 50 g ball:
55% viscose, 33% cotton, 12% linen
[CYCA 2]

Rowan Savannah
87 yd. (80 m) per 50 g ball:
94% cotton, 6% silk [CYCA 4]

Rowan Wool Cotton
123 yd. (113 m) per 50 g ball:
50% merino wool, 50% cotton [CYCA 3]

**Wensleydale Longwool Sheepshop
Hand-Dyed Fleece**
100% Wensleydale wool [CYCA 6]

Standard Yarn Weight System

Yarn Weight Symbol and Category Name	Super Fine 1	Fine 2	Light 3	Medium 4	Bulky 5	Super Bulky 6
Types of yarn in category	Sock, fingering, baby	Sport, baby	DK, light worsted	Worsted, afghan, Aran	Chunky, craft, rug	Bulky, roving
Knit gauge range in St st in 4 in.*	27–32 sts	23–26 sts	21–24 sts	16–20 sts	12–15 sts	6–11 sts
Recommended metric needle size	2.25–3.25 mm	3.25–3.75 mm	3.75–4.5 mm	4.5–5.5 mm	5.5–8 mm	8 mm and larger
Recommended U.S. needle size	1–3	3–5	5–7	7–9	9–11	11 and larger
Crochet gauge range in sc in 4 in.*	21–31 sts	16–20 sts	12–17 sts	11–14 sts	8–11 sts	5–9 sts
Recommended metric hook size	2.25–3.5 mm	3.5–4.5 mm	4.5–5.5 mm	5.5–6.5 mm	6.5–9 mm	9 mm and larger
Recommended U.S. hook size	B/1–E/4	E/4–7	7–I/9	I/9–K/10.5	K/10.5–M/13	M/13 and larger

*The information in this table reflects the most commonly used gauges
  and needle or hook sizes for the specific yarn categories.

~~~~~~~~~~~~~~~~~~~~~~~~~~~~

Buttons and Trimmings

BEAUTIFUL BUTTONS, FASTENERS, AND TRIMMINGS can add a "wow" factor to any garment. My favorites are made of glass, mother-of-pearl, silver, copper, and ceramic. I'm always on the lookout for unusual handcrafted buttons and love vintage buttons. Also, the idea of recycling old ones from secondhand sweaters bought for practically nothing in thrift shops really appeals to me. I usually prefer shank buttons to those with holes because it's easier to focus on the design of the button.

Color is important when choosing buttons and trimmings, and if you can't get an exact match to the yarn, it's better to go for a complete contrast. Also consider scale when buying buttons. The balance of the garment will be thrown out of kilter if you get this wrong. For example, a bold design in chunky yarn will need big buttons to complement the design, but a fine silk yarn will never look elegant with heavy wooden buttons dragging it down—delicate mother-of-pearl buttons would work better.

Never scrimp on trimmings; choose them carefully to complement your project, which has taken lots of your valuable time to knit. If you just can't find what you're looking for, consider making your own. Knots or bobbles will work as fasteners for some projects, and you can always buy button blanks and cover them with knitted fabric.

Knitting Abbreviations

alt   alternate

approx   approximately

beg   beginning

ch   chain (single crochet)

cn   cable needle

cm(s)   centimeter(s)

cont   continue

dec   decrease

dpn(s)   double-pointed needle(s)

ev   every

g   grams

in.   inch(es)

inc   increase

k   knit

k2tog   knit 2 sts together

k3tog   knit 3 sts together

kfb   knit st in front and back

kwise   knitwise

LH   left hand

m   meter(s)

m1   knit in front and back of this st

mm   millimeter(s)

p   purl

p2tog   purl 2 sts together

p3tog   purl 3 sts together

p3tog-b   p2tog, then slip stitch back onto LH needle. Using RH needle pass the next stitch beyond over this stitch, then slip the same stitch back to RH needle again and continue.

pm   place marker

psso   pass slipped st over

ptog-b   p2tog through back of loops

rep   repeat

rem   remaining

RH   right hand

RS   right side

s2kpo   sl2tog kwise, k1, pass 2 slipped sts over

sk   skip

sk2po   slip 1 st wyib, k2tog, psso

skpo   slip 1 st, k1, pass the slipped st over

sl   slip

sl2tog   slip 2 sts together

sm   slip marker

ssk   (slip, slip, knit)—slip next 2 sts knitwise, one at a time, to RH needle. Insert tip of LH needle into fronts of these sts from left to right and knit them together.

st(s)   stitch(es)

tbl   through back loop

tog   together

w & t   wrap yarn and turn work

WS   wrong side

wyib   with yarn in back

yd.   yard(s)

yo   yarn over needle to make 1 st

Needle and Hook Sizing

Knitting Needles

Millimeter Range	U.S. Size Range
2.25 mm	1
2.75 mm	2
3.25 mm	3
3.5 mm	4
3.75 mm	5
4 mm	6
4.5 mm	7
5 mm	8
5.5 mm	9
6 mm	10
6.5 mm	10½
8 mm	11
9 mm	13
10 mm	15
12.75 mm	17
15 mm	19
19 mm	35
25 mm	50

Crochet Hooks

Millimeter Range	U.S. Size Range
2.25 mm	B-1
2.75 mm	C-2
3.25 mm	D-3
3.5 mm	E-4
3.75 mm	F-5
4 mm	G-6
4.5 mm	7
5 mm	H-8
5.5 mm	I-9
6 mm	J-10
6.5 mm	K-10½
8 mm	L-11
9 mm	M/N-13
10 mm	N/P-15
15 mm	P/Q
16 mm	Q
19 mm	S

Project Index

Cuddle Cocoon, p. 8

Shower Set, p. 12

Baby Love Blanket, p. 16

Whoopla Beanbags, p. 20

Jubilee Jacket and Hat, p. 24

Fiesta Shrug and Fingerless Gloves, p. 36

Jive Leg Warmers, p. 38

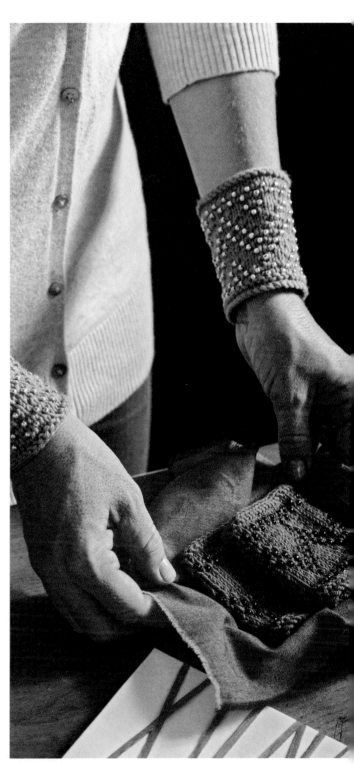

Glow Wristlets, p. 40

Froufrou Fingerless Gloves, p. 42

Amulet Purse, p. 46

Deco Backpack, p. 50

Will-o'-the-Wisp Shawlette, p. 54

Galaxy Beret, p. 59

Kitten's Paw Stole, p. 62

Odalisque Turban and Hat, p. 66

Zebra Mittens, p. 69

Hugs Socks, p. 74

Masham Scarf, p. 78

Galway Beanie and Head Wrap, p. 82

Tutti-Frutti Smartphone Sleeve, p. 85

Hendrix Guitar Strap and Linen Belt, p. 88

Checkers Cushion and Seat Cover, p. 94

Flavor Place Mat and Napkin Ring, p. 100

Wensleydale Tea Cozy, p. 104

McDougal Dog Jacket, p. 108

Welcome Toran Door Hanging, p. 113

APPENDIX VII

Index

About the Author

JEAN MOSS IS ONE OF Britain's leading knitwear designers. Her innovative combinations of intricate textures, striking colorways, and sophisticated styling have been widely influential in the global knitting community.

A self-taught knitwear designer, Jean produced her own unique collections of handknits for many years, which were sold in the United States, Japan, and Europe. In the 1980s and 1990s, Jean also worked on design and production for many international fashion houses, such as Polo Ralph Lauren, Laura Ashley, and Benetton. Currently, her designs are featured regularly in *Rowan Knitting and Crochet Magazine, The Knitter*, and *Vogue Knitting,* and for six years she hosted "Ask Jean," an advice column in the U.K. magazine *Knitting.*

Jean is passionate about good design and has always believed that it should be available to all who appreciate it, not just the few who can afford to buy couture. *Great Little Gifts to Knit* is her 11th book of handknit designs, the most recent being *Sweet Shawlettes* (The Taunton Press).

Jean's other passions include gardening, music, and vegetarian food. Her personal take on color, texture, shape, and form is expressed in the one-off, imaginative gardens she designs for clients in North Yorkshire, England. Music plays a big part in her life, and her album *More Yarn Will Do the Trick* is a trio of textile-related songs.

For the past decade, Jean and her partner, Philip, have hosted knitting and garden tours in the United Kingdom, which have become so successful that they are now going further afield to exotic locations such as Morocco and Greece. She loves to meet other knitters and travels extensively, teaching workshops in both the United States and Europe. For more information on Jean's books, patterns, kits, ready-to-wear, workshops, lectures, and tours, visit www.jeanmoss.com.

If you like this book, you'll love everything about *Threads*.